Caribbean
Dependence on
the United States
Economy

CARIBBEAN
DEPENDENCE ON
THE UNITED STATES
ECONOMY

Ransford W. Palmer

PRAEGER PUBLISHERS
Praeger Special Studies

New York • London • Sydney • Toronto

Library of Congress Cataloging in Publication Data

Palmer, Ransford W
    Caribbean dependence on the United States economy.

    Bibliography: p.
    1. United States--Foreign economic relations--
Caribbean area. 2. Caribbean area--Foreign
economic relations--United States. 3. Caribbean
area--Economic conditions. I. Title.
HF1456.5.C27P34 1979   330.9'729   78-19770
    ISBN 0-03-041426-1

PRAEGER PUBLISHERS, PRAEGER SPECIAL STUDIES
383 Madison Avenue, New York, N.Y., 10017, U.S.A.

Published in the United States of America in 1979
by Praeger Publishers,
A Division of Holt, Rinehart and Winston, CBS Inc.

9 038   987654321

© 1979 by Praeger Publishers

Printed in the United States of America

To my wife Sally and my children,
Geoffrey, Christopher, and Laura

Acknowledgments

The preparation of the manuscript for this book was facilitated by a grant from the Faculty Research Program in Social Sciences, Humanities, and Education at Howard University (through the Office of the Vice President for Academic Affairs) and by a Faculty Research Fellowship from the Howard University Department of Economics.

A number of people provided me with useful sources of information. Among them are Michael Alleyne, Terrence R. Colvin, Murchison Henry, Vincent R. McDonald, and Judy Sever. Graduate students Fatemeh Ali-Nejadfard, Ravinder Aulakh, Ephraim Mbaba, and Lakhbir Singh provided research assistance at various stages of the development of the manuscript.

I am grateful to Surinder Gujral for allowing me to intrude freely upon his time with some of my ideas and to Reynold Madoo for comments on a preliminary version of part of this work.

I am particularly indebted to my wife, Sally, for her valuable editorial comments and for typing numerous drafts of the manuscript.

While I am pleased to acknowledge the assistance of all those mentioned, I am solely responsible for the contents of this book.

Contents

LIST OF TABLES AND FIGURES

Table   Page

LIST OF ABBREVIATIONS

ACP	African, Caribbean, and Pacific (nations, cosigners of the Lomé Convention)
AID	Agency for International Development
ARP	average realized price
bpd	barrels per day
BWICLO	British West Indies Central Labor Organization
CARICOM	Caribbean Community
CARIFTA	Caribbean Free Trade Area
CDB	Caribbean Development Bank
CDF	Caribbean Development Facility
EEC	European Economic Community
FAO	Food and Agricultural Organization
f.a.s.	free alongside ship
GDP	Gross Domestic Product
GNP	Gross National Product
GSP	Generalized System of Preferences
IBA	International Bauxite Association
IBRD	International Bank for Reconstruction and Development
IDB	Inter-American Development Bank
IFAD	International Fund for Agricultural Development
IMF	International Monetary Fund
JBI	Jamaica Bauxite Institute
LDT	long dry ton
NACLA	North American Congress on Latin America
N.A.	Not Available
ODA	Official Development Assistance
OECD	Organisation for Economic Co-operation and Development
OPEC	Organization of Petroleum Exporting Countries
PTK	Professional, Technical, and Kindred
SITC	Standard International Trade Classification
ST	short ton
UNCTAD	United Nations Conference on Trade and Development
UNDP	United Nations Development Programme
USDA	United States Department of Agriculture

✦ Caribbean
✦ Dependence on
✦ the United States
✦ Economy

I

Introduction

A common characteristic of all Caribbean economies is their economic and financial dependence on one metropolitan country or another.

This study examines the nature of the dependence of the four major English-speaking Caribbean countries—Jamaica, Trinidad and Tobago, Guyana, and Barbados—upon the economy of the United States. The short histories of these countries as independent nations provide an ideal example of the shifting, within the international capitalist system, of their economic dependence from one metropolitan center to another. Although one could argue that the shift began during World War II, when the United States acquired strategic military bases in the Caribbean through lend-lease arrangements with Great Britain, the growth of its visible economic form accelerated during the 1960s when large-scale U.S. direct investment poured into the growth points of the region.[1]

These Caribbean countries became politically independent during that decade which marked a period of one of the longest and most impressive economic expansions experienced by the United States after World War II. Multinational firms, anxious to secure cheap and stable sources of raw materials, invested heavily in the mineral industries of the Caribbean. The subsequent expansion of mineral output in those countries was largely responsible for the dramatic growth of Caribbean trade with the United States, leading in turn to the establishment of the United States as the most important trading partner of the region.

While trade with the United States grew rapidly, the Caribbean development strategy of industrialization by invitation inspired by W. Arthur Lewis[2] failed to develop a viable manufacturing sector that would create adequate employment opportunities for an expanding work force. The assumption that

TABLE 1.1

Per Capita Gross Domestic Product
(U.S. $, current and 1970 prices)

Year	Jamaica		Trinidad and Tobago		Guyana		Barbados		United States[*]	
	Current Prices	1970 Prices	Current Prices	1970 Prices	Current Prices	1970 Prices	Current Prices	1970 Prices	Current Prices	1970 Prices
1970	763	763	791	790	373	373	615	615	4,795	4,795
1971	826	788	871	800	365	361	679	604	5,136	4,887
1972	905	826	970	820	398	375	738	613	5,607	5,123
1973	1,056	805	1,162	873	479	420	861	612	6,210	5,362
1974	1,334	818	1,687	1,056	589	440	1,178	603	6,668	5,251
1975	1,548	808	2,159	1,147	736	509	1,374	585	7,159	5,143
1976	1,594	760	2,396	1,183	580	368	1,469	599	7,933	5,413

[*]Per capita gross national product.

Sources: Trinidad and Tobago Ministry of Finance (Planning and Development), *The Gross Domestic Product of the Republic of Trinidad & Tobago 1966–1976* (Port of Spain: Central Statistical Office, 1977); Jamaica Department of Statistics, *National Income and Product 1976* (Kingston: Department of Statistics, 1977); International Monetary Fund, *International Financial Statistics* 30 (1977); Barbados Economic Planning Unit, *Economic Survey 1968; 1971* (Bridgetown: Government Printing Office, 1969, 1972).

foreign capital was indispensable for development because poor countries could not generate enough savings to finance their capital needs led Caribbean development policy to be preoccupied with granting state favors to induce the inflow of foreign direct investment. Yet long after the foreign capital arrived, incomes in these developing countries remained relatively low while unemployment remained high, and substantial savings outflows in the form of repatriated profits went to metropolitan countries.

Although the nominal values of aggregate economic indexes indicate impressive growth in the Caribbean economies, the real values give a different picture. Table 1.1 shows that in 1976 real per capita gross domestic product (GDP) at 1970 prices was lower than it was in 1970 for all countries with the exception of Trinidad and Tobago which registered substantial growth during the entire period.[*]

---

[*]Unless otherwise indicated, all monetary figures are given in U.S. dollars throughout this work. Conversion into U.S. dollars is based on the par rate of exchange for each Caribbean currency.

To a large extent, external events were responsible for these diverse performances. Principal among them was the dramatic increase in the cost of oil in 1973, which benefited Trinidad and Tobago and devastated Jamaica. Sharp declines in the prices of major export commodities since the latter part of 1975 combined with uncertain domestic political conditions and high import propensities to precipitate a serious balance-of-payments crisis for the non-oil-producing countries. Between 1970 and 1976, the growth of GDP of the region was due largely to inflation which since 1973 has been hovering around 20 percent a year for all the countries. Needless to say, this has had a negative impact on the distribution of income which was highly unequal to begin with.

By standards of developing countries, the per capita GDP figures shown in Table 1.1 are high. Yet in 1976 the figures in real values for Barbados and Guyana were only 11.0 percent and 6.7 percent, respectively, of the U.S. per capita GDP. For Jamaica and Trinidad and Tobago, the respective figures were 14.0 percent and 21.8 percent. Thus, after more than a decade of political independence and foreign-capital-dependent development effort, the gap between the Caribbean and the United States has remained wide—and for three countries it has grown wider.

In 1976 the four Caribbean countries under consideration had a total population of 4.3 million, which has been growing at an annual rate of 1.8 percent since 1966. The labor force has grown younger and more urban in the process. In Jamaica, for example, the 1976 population was a little over 2 million; the share of those under 20 increased from 51.7 percent in 1960 to 53.1 percent in 1976, and the urban population moved from 33.6 to 41.4 percent between the 1960 and 1970 censuses. While the share of the Jamaican labor force under the age of 24 rose from 26 to 28 percent, the growth of job opportunities at the unskilled and semiskilled end of the employment spectrum has not kept pace. The consequence is that the already high national unemployment rates that, in 1976, exceeded 20 percent, mask the astronomical unemployment rates within the younger age groups. The slow growth of economic opportunities together with other factors force many would-be workers to migrate to the metropole to realize their expectations, long conditioned by exposure to metropolitan consumption standards. Thus the metropole becomes the new urban sector where income levels are higher and economic opportunities perceived to be greater.

The viability of the Caribbean minieconomies in this last quarter of the twentieth century is in doubt. Individually, their pursuit of national development has made them more open—that is, the ratio of their exports plus imports to gross domestic product has generally grown larger—and therefore more vulnerable to external shocks generated within the metropole. To arrest this drift toward greater dependence, a regional approach to development has been espoused. The creation of the Caribbean Free Trade Area (CARIFTA) in 1968 and its expansion into the Caribbean Community (CARICOM) in 1973 is an important step toward the eventual economic integration of the region. This approach has been selected as the most realistic political alternative to combat dependence on the metropole, despite the stumbling blocks of national sovereignty that will be encountered along this path.

This work deals essentially with the four major facets of Caribbean dependence on the U.S. economy: trade dependence, financial dependence, dependence on emigration, and the dependence of local economic policies engendered by the above.

In Chapter 2, "The Caribbean Quest for Economic Power," the attempt of Caribbean governments to rearrange the traditional ownership pattern of investment in the "commanding heights" of their economies will be examined. Chapter 3, "Caribbean Trade Dependence on the United States," underscores the relationship between direct investment by the United States in the Caribbean and Caribbean trade with the United States. Principal exports and imports will be examined with a view toward illuminating the nature of the trade dependence. Chapter 4, "Dependence and Economic Stability," focuses on the critical problem of the effectiveness of economic stabilization policies in small open developing Caribbean economies.

Chapter 5, "Dependence and Foreign Capital Flows," looks at the change in the structure of capital inflows from a predominance of equity capital to a predominance of debt capital and the implications of the resultant growth of the public debt. It also examines the paradoxical situation of the capital-poor Caribbean as net supplier of capital to the United States. Chapter 6, "Migration of Human Resources to the United States," provides a detailed analysis of the significance of migration from the Caribbean to the United States since the early 1960s. Finally, Chapter 7, "Caribbean Development and U.S. Policy," examines the two major issues that are likely to affect U.S. policy toward development in the region: the call for a new international economic order and economic cooperation in the Caribbean.

Appendix A, "Getting Control of a Commanding Height: The Jamaican Bauxite Industry," discusses the transformation of ownership and control of the bauxite operations and the problem of integrating the industry into the local economy. Appendix B, "U.S. Consumption of Caribbean Tourism," provides an analysis of the implications of U.S. economic growth for the Caribbean tourist industry. Appendix C, "An Empirical Analysis of Caribbean Migration to the United States," provides a theoretical and empirical analysis of Caribbean migration to the United States.

NOTES

1. Pinto and Kñakal observe that this shift of center-periphery relationship has

serious implications for the functioning of the world economy in general, and Centre-Periphery relations in particular. Since investment is the chief autonomous determinant of U.S. economic activity, the sensitivity of its economy to external stimuli—for increasing exports, as well as its capacity to "return them" to other countries through increases in imports—seemed much less than in the case of Great Britain, the former centre.

Aníbal Pinto and Jan Kñakal, "The Centre-Periphery System Twenty Years Later," *Social and Economic Studies* 22 (1973): 35.

2. W. Arthur Lewis, "The Industrialization of the British West Indies," *Caribbean Economic Review*, 1950.

2

The Caribbean Quest for Economic Power

In this chapter we will examine the attempt of the Commonwealth Caribbean—particularly Jamaica and Guyana—to create new strategies for national development in order to alter their traditional economic relationship with the developed capitalist world—the United States, in particular.

NEW GOALS AND NEW STRATEGIES

The general thrust of the new strategies in the Commonwealth Caribbean is to achieve two primary goals: to reduce the extreme dependence on the metropole; and to retain for local development a larger share of the economic surplus produced by locally based foreign enterprises.

Because Caribbean economies are typically dominated by one or two major primary industries—most of whose products are exported to the United States or the United Kingdom—Caribbean policy makers have generally accepted the proposition that the diversification of both production and markets will reduce dependence on metropolitan economies. The diversification of production usually means the establishment of a wide range of manufacturing activities, while diversification of markets essentially means the expansion of exports to the European Common Market, Russia, Eastern Europe, and Japan and other Asian countries, as well as to other countries of the Caribbean.*

---

*The creation of CARIFTA in 1968 and its development into CARICOM five years later was an effort in this direction.

Market diversification also means securing a wider source of imports. This may be more difficult to accomplish than finding additional markets for export, since the import of consumption goods may be closely tied with local cultures— tastes and preferences which have developed over long periods. Food, for example, presents a special problem, because the Caribbean is highly dependent on the import of staples such as wheat and corn, most of which come from the United States.*

In order to achieve the goal of retaining for local development a larger share of the profits of the locally based foreign enterprise, Caribbean governments have focused their attention on the critical role of foreign corporations in the Caribbean economy. There has been a general dissatisfaction with the contribution of the multinational corporation to the social and economic development of the region under traditional ownership arrangements. Further-more, the fact that major economic decisions affecting the Caribbean are made externally in the boardrooms of these corporations is perceived as undermining the sovereignty of the Caribbean nations.[1] Trinidad's perception of the problem is typical: " . . . vital economic decisions affecting the country's economy have been taken externally . . . by metropolitan Governments and metropolitan producers. . . . In short, the economy has been acted upon, with the local Governments and people playing a passive dependent role in the process."[2]

These countries are now actively rearranging the balance between their national interest and private foreign corporate interest as a necessary first step toward retaining a larger share of profits for local development. This rearrange-ment is being manifested in policies of wholesale nationalization of foreign firms in Guyana as well as in joint-venture arrangements in Jamaica and Trinidad and Tobago.

Guyana declared itself a Cooperative Republic in 1970. Since then, it has gone farther in the direction of state ownership and control of production than any other Caribbean country. Following the 1971 nationalization of the Demerara Bauxite Company, a wholly owned subsidiary of the Canadian company Alcan, Guyana nationalized all major foreign-owned firms including the American-owned Reynolds Mines (in 1975).[3] Some 80 percent of economic activity in Guyana is under state control. The creation of a Ministry of Public Corporations in December 1970 to rationalize the administration of the growing number of public corporations is part of the new bureaucracy which national-ization has engendered.[4]

Prime Minister Michael Manley of Jamaica argues persuasively that "political independence and national sovereignty are inconsistent with a situation in which the 'commanding heights' of the economy are foreign-owned and controlled."[5] But instead of across-the-board nationalization, Jamaica has,

---

*The problem will be discussed at length in Chapter 3.

for the most part, taken the joint-venture approach, acquiring majority ownership in the bauxite operations.*

This prevailing attitude regarding domestic ownership and control of productive resources is in contrast to that of the early and middle 1960s when the Caribbean countries became politically independent. At that time, each country made a special effort to woo private foreign capital, especially U.S. capital. A special independence supplement in the New York *Times* extolling the opportunities for private investment and the security of stable political conditions was a sine qua non of Caribbean coming-out celebrations. And in the development plans that followed independence, the attitude toward the private sector, and particularly toward foreign investment, was extremely accommodating.

Guyana's Development Programme 1966–1972, to cite one example, clearly espoused industrialization by invitation to build "a vigorous economic democracy which is not a copy of either Eastern Communism or Western Capitalism."[6] In addition to displaying the usual range of industrial tax incentives—income-tax holidays, tariff concessions, and the like—the Guyana government declared its willingness to encourage foreign investors by proclaiming: "An agreement has been entered into with the Government of the United States of America to guarantee the investments made by American investors in Guyana. Guyana thus becomes part of that area in which the U.S. government feels that its nationals can invest with confidence."[7]

Although the Programme hinted at a "need for a policy of Government's active participation in pioneering investment,"[8] it made it crystal clear that

> the objective of the Government is neither to obtain control of private industries nor to gain direct participation in their profits through substantial equity holdings. The aim is to remove obstacles to rapid industrial development by providing pre-investment and other promotional services and where necessary to participate financially to ensure that desirable industries can be started.[9]

Today the objective of the government of Guyana has changed dramatically. The country has transformed itself into a socialist state with almost total control of its domestic commercial enterprises.[10]

In Jamaica, the major shift in postindependence economic strategy came in 1972 when the Manley government came to power. Though more moderate than the Guyanese philosophy, Jamaica's policy is essentially a shift from a development strategy relying heavily on the private sector to a more controlled

---

*For a detailed discussion of Jamaica's drive to own and control its bauxite industry, see Appendix A, "Getting Control of a Commanding Height: The Jamaican Bauxite Industry."

economy in which the state becomes the major instrument for mobilizing resources for development.*

INTERNATIONAL CONSTRAINTS ON THE NEW STRATEGIES

The mere acquisition of local ownership and control of multinational corporations in the Caribbean will not necessarily make these economies less dependent on the metropole if the acquired local operations continue to produce primary inputs for a vertically integrated multinational corporate structure which in turn produces for metropolitan and Caribbean consumption. If domestic ownership and control is to reduce that kind of dependence, there must be an integration of the primary industries into the local economies through the development of new linkages.

Further, the transfer of the locus of decision making from the foreign-based multinational firm to the local government in no way insulates the Caribbean from the actions taken by metropolitan governments to protect the investments of their multinational firms. Guyana is a case in point. It relies heavily upon the World Bank for long-term funds to develop important infrastructure. C. H. Grant claims that because of the interest shown by the United States in the 1971 nationalization of the Demerara Bauxite Company, whose Canadian parent corporation Alcan has the "majority of [its] shares . . . located in the United States," and the precedent such nationalization would set for the American firm, Reynolds Bauxite Company (which was in fact nationalized in 1975), pressure was put on Guyana by the World Bank "to reach an amicable agreement on the compensation issues."[11]

The United States, as the largest contributor to the World Bank, is in a position to affect Bank policies. "In the same way that it cut off bilateral development aid to Peru in the 1960's to back up an embattled American firm, the United States would not hesitate to apply pressure on the World Bank to act as a champion of the foreign investor. . . ."[12]

The World Bank exercises its influence through its lending policies which, as E. V. K. Fitzgerald argues, tends to reinforce the dependence of developing countries on the metropole: "the influence of the international agencies (which in their turn act as 'chairmen' and 'inspectors' for the capitalist bloc) is such as to reinforce the dependence upon foreign capital goods and technology on the one hand, and the confining of public enterprise activity to an 'infrastructural' role on the other."[13]

---

*A discussion of some of the economic implications of this shift can be found in Chapters 4 and 5.

TOWARD AN INDUSTRIALLY DIVERSIFIED FUTURE

Despite these constraints, the general thrust of economic policies in the Commonwealth Caribbean today is clearly one that seeks to transform those economies from a status of dependence to one of diversified industrial production. The proposition that such a transition can come about only if there is a national will to restructure internal institutional arrangements governing production and consumption has gained wide acceptance. What is more, the dramatic increase in the role of the state has come to be regarded as the manifestation of that will. Thus Caribbean governments, socialist and capitalist alike, strive for greater ownership of domestic productive resources and the control of the allocation of them into diversified economic activities chosen as desirable by the state. The kind of laissez-faire openness typical of the Caribbean economies in the 1950s and 1960s—the era of industrialization by invitation—is rapidly being replaced by domination by state institutions and the new bureaucracies those institutions spawn.

Whatever the name given to the new political economy, be it cooperative republicanism or democratic socialism, the major source of national income for the Caribbean for some time to come will continue to be the major export industries: sugar, bauxite, oil refining, and tourism. Therefore, national and regional policies designed to improve the efficiency of production and marketing of these products will provide the basic assurance for greater gains from trade in the future. In addition, policies designed to broaden the base of the primary industries to include a wider range of local ancillary industries will contribute directly not only to the retention of larger savings for local and regional development, but also to building the foundation for a truly self-generating industrial economic base. The import substitution strategy embraced by the Caribbean countries in the 1950s and 1960s has not been successful in forming a self-generating industrial economic base, simply because the export industries were not made an integral part of the strategy. Any new plan for industrial development must utilize the foreign exchange generated by the raw-material-producing export industries to develop industrial linkages which can utilize those raw materials.

The Caribbean, in all likelihood, will continue to depend on foreign capital for a long time to come. But the character of that foreign capital is likely to become increasingly "public and institutional rather than private."[14] With perhaps the exception of Guyana, the joint-venture approach by Caribbean governments to private foreign investment will undoubtedly continue to be an important part of this process, just as it has been an integral feature of development policy in many Latin American countries for a long time. But this approach, too, is not without its problems. After observing the joint-venture experience in Latin America, Roy Blough and Jack Behrman warn that restrictive measures affecting the operations of foreign enterprise, such as rigid requirements for joint ventures with local private capital or with state enterprises, could limit substantially the participation of foreign private capital in the [Latin American] integration effort, with a correspondent reduction in the contribution of capital, technology, and management by foreign investors.[15]

Fitzgerald has also observed that

in the case of joint ventures, which are becoming increasingly important in heavy industry, transport and tourism, the [Latin American] state is essentially buying technology and capital goods—in return for guaranteed profits and monopoly markets—and it is here, if anywhere, that dependency is strengthened.[16]

Despite these problems, the importance of joint-venturing is recognized as a means to enable a country to achieve control over the actions of the multinationals and, more importantly, to direct the flow of capital, technology, and management and marketing know-how into targeted areas for development. Whether the strategy is one of nationalization or joint-venturing, the essential point being made by Caribbean governments is that the quest for economic power cannot be successful without effective control of the economic decision-making process.

NOTES

1. The nature of the political problem which corporate power creates is probably best expressed by John Kenneth Galbraith: "When the modern corporation acquires power over markets, power in the community, power over the state, power over belief, it is a political instrument, different in form and degree but not in kind from the state itself." "Power and the Useful Economist," *American Economic Review* 63 (1973): 6.

2. Trinidad and Tobago, *Third Five-Year Plan 1969–1973 (Draft)* (Port-of-Spain: Government Printery, 1969), p. 7.

3. Ralph R. Premdas describes the events leading up to the nationalization of the Reynolds Bauxite Company:

The government opened talks with Reynolds on July 10, 1974, for majority participation. The company's reply was that it was willing to pay back taxes of nearly $3.5 million (U.S.) but demanded that future taxes were not to be related to increased prices for bauxite, and the government must abandon nationalization intentions and other forms of participation for five years. The talks broke down. On September 25, 1974, the government legislatively imposed a bauxite levy on Reynolds under which the company was required to pay $6 million (U.S.), half of which was due within 15 days. Reynolds refused to pay, took the government to court for breach of contract, lost, retrenched workers, repatriated overseas staff, and so on, and eventually the government nationalized the company.

"Guyana: Socialist Reconstruction or Political Opportunism?" *Journal of Interamerican Studies and World Affairs* 20 (1978): 147.

4. See Ethlyn Prince, "The Development of Public Enterprise in Guyana," *Social and Economic Studies* 23 (1974): 204–15.

5. Michael Manley, *The Politics of Change: A Jamaican Testament* (Washington, D.C.: Howard University Press, 1975), p. 115.

6. Guyana, *British Guiana (Guyana) Development Programme 1966–1972* (Georgetown: The Government Printery, 1966), p. vii.

7. Ibid., p. III–5.

8. Ibid., p. XV–5.

9. Ibid.

10. According to Premdas, op. cit., p. 138:

Perhaps no other single factor explains the ideological about change in [Guyana's Prime Minister Forbes] Burnham after 1970 better than [his] obsession with his international reputation. . . . Note, for example, how every act of nationalization was widely publicized by the regime as was the steady stream of dignitaries visiting Guyana including Fidel Castro, Julius Nyrere, and Madam Bandaranaike. Burnham himself was hosted by the court of Mao Tse-tung, while Guyana sponsored several international conferences and festivals at great cost to herself. The upshot was that Guyana's image as a backward client state of western imperialism governed by a supine and submissive government gradually shifted so that Burnham acquired a reputation himself as a progressive Third World Leader.

But Premdas (pp. 161–62) also asserts that "the nationalization of foreign firms in Guyana originated from economic necessity. Socialist principles involved post facto to justify nationalizations later became the determinative guide in government decision-making."

Jay R. Mandle argues that in order for the Burnham government to extend its nationalization efforts into the sphere of sugar, it had to win the support of the East Indian population:

Thus the Burnham Government by the mid-1970s confronted a major choice: If it proposed to address seriously the question of integrating the Guyanese economy, it was compelled to reorganize sugar. But to do so necessitated its enlisting the goodwill of the East Indian population. In the Guyanese context this could only mean reaching an understanding with the [People's Progressive Party] and in particular with Cheddi Jagan. For it is only Jagan, as the still charismatic leader, who possesses the power to mobilize this segment of the Guyanese population.

"Continuity and Change in Guyanese Underdevelopment," *Revista/Review Interamericana* 7 (1977): 225.

11. C. H. Grant, "Political Sequence to Alcan Nationalization in Guyana—The International Aspects," *Social and Economic Studies* 22 (1973): 267–68.

12. Ibid., p. 266.

13. E. V. K. Fitzgerald, "Some Aspects of the Political Economy of the Latin American State," *Development and Change* 7 (1976): 127.

14. Manley, op. cit., p. 116.

15. Roy Blough and Jack N. Behrman, "Problems of Regional Integration in Latin America," in *Regional Integration and the Trade of Latin America* ed. Committee for Economic Development (New York: Committee for Economic Development, 1968), p. 42.

16. Fitzgerald, op. cit., p. 127.

3

Caribbean Trade Dependence on the United States

The U.S. view of its economic relationship with the Caribbean as one of interdependency is based on the following points: [1]

Two-thirds of the U.S. requirements of bauxite/alumina come from the Caribbean;

One-fourth of the U.S. petroleum imports are refined or transhipped in the Caribbean;

U.S. exports to the Caribbean total $2 billion annually; and

Direct private U.S. investment in the area is estimated to be $4.3 billion.

Viewed from the Caribbean, these figures reflect the high degree to which Caribbean economies are locked into the larger U.S. economy. The large volume of U.S. private investment is the fulcrum on which U.S.-Caribbean trade relationships rest. It is responsible for the large share of Caribbean bauxite, alumina, and petroleum exports to the United States; a substantial share of Caribbean imports from the United States go to U.S.-owned firms.

Because Caribbean trade with the United States is in such a large measure related to U.S. investment in the Caribbean, this chapter will begin with a survey of the scope and structure of this investment. It will then discuss the structure of Caribbean trade with the United States, focusing on the principal categories of traded products. It will also look at the evolution of Caribbean trade with the periphery, for example, CARICOM and Latin America, highlighting the fact that although the Caribbean is primarily an exporter of raw materials and semiprocessed goods to the United States, it is also a major importer of raw materials from the periphery. Finally, it will assess the problem of trade and dependence. An empirical analysis of the implications of the growth of U.S. consumption of Caribbean tourist services is conducted in Appendix B.

DIRECT INVESTMENT BY THE UNITED STATES

The behavior of direct investment by the United States between 1966 and 1976 in the four countries is shown in Table 3.1. While total U.S. direct investment has grown from under $0.5 billion in 1966 to $1.3 billion in 1976, it is the behavior of U.S. investment in the individual countries that is revealing. In Guyana and Jamaica, for example, U.S. direct investment declined in the 1970s, reflecting the adoption of new socialist strategies for development in 1970 (Guyana) and 1972 (Jamaica). By 1976, U.S. direct investment in Guyana was half of what it was in 1970 when the new Cooperative Republic embarked upon a policy of wholesale nationalization of foreign enterprises. In Jamaica in 1976, investment by the United States was $50 million less than in 1972 when the new government of Michael Manley began to steer the island on a path of democratic socialism embodying the ideal of local ownership and control of the economy's "commanding heights."

The growth of U.S. investment in Trinidad was negligible between 1966 and 1972, but it accelerated from $280 million in 1972 to $713 million in 1976.

TABLE 3.1

U.S. Direct Investment in the Caribbean at Year End, 1966–76 ($ million)

Year	Barbados	Guyana	Trinidad and Tobago	Jamaica
1966	3	N.A.	207	163
1967	3	N.A.	217	204
1968	6	40	215	295
1969	6	40	185	392
1970	9	40	198	507
1971	12	35	262	618
1972	18	36	280	624
1973	20	–	433	618
1974	20	20	549	609
1975	19	22	656	654
1976	20	21	713	577

Note: Investment is at net book value.
Source: U.S. Department of Commerce, Bureau of Economic Analysis.

TABLE 3.2

Foreign and U.S. Direct Investment in Trinidad and Tobago, 1969–74
($ million)

Year	Assets of the Foreign Capital Sector (1)	U.S. Direct Investment (2)	2 as a Percent of 1
1969	241.2	185.0	76.7
1970	286.1	198.0	69.2
1971	343.9	262.0	76.2
1972	417.6	280.0	67.0
1973	601.8	433.0	71.9
1974	737.9	549.0	74.4

Source: Flow of Funds for Trinidad and Tobago 1966–1974 (Port-of-Spain: Central Statistical Office, 1977); U.S. Department of Commerce, Bureau of International Investment.

This jump was induced by the sharp increase in world petroleum prices in 1973 and by the pragmatic commitment of the government of Trinidad and Tobago to a capitalist course of development. At least 90 percent of direct investment by the United States in Trinidad and Tobago is in the petroleum industry. This investment accounted for over 70 percent of the assets of the foreign corporate sector in Trinidad between 1969 and 1974 (see Table 3.2).

U.S. direct investment in Barbados is small. Starting from a mere $3 million in 1966, it reached a peak of $20 million in 1973 and remained there up to 1976.

Despite the decline of U.S. investment in Jamaica and that government's recent acquisition of majority ownership of the major American bauxite firms (see Appendix A), such investment remains an important factor in the Jamaican economy. The major share of this investment is in the mining industry which in 1976 accounted for 66 percent of the value of domestic exports. Table 3.3 shows the distribution of U.S. direct investment by industrial sector in Jamaica for 1975 and 1976, and Table 3.4 shows the composition of foreign and local sales by majority-owned foreign affiliates of U.S. companies in Jamaica in 1975.

From Table 3.4 it is clear that almost all of the products of the mining firms (bauxite) are exported and that most of the products of the manufacturing firms are sold locally. For all industries, sales made abroad accounted for 52 percent of total sales, and 66 percent of the sales abroad are made to the United States. The mining firms themselves accounted for 93 percent of the sales to the United States. Altogether, in 1975, the export sales of majority-owned foreign affiliates of U.S. companies in Jamaica represented 50 percent of Jamaica's domestic exports

TABLE 3.3

Distribution of U.S. Direct Investment in Jamaica at Year End, 1975–76
($ million)

Item	1975	1976
Mining and smelting ⎱	390	302
Petroleum ⎰		38
Manufacturing	219	226
Trade	8	8
Finance and insurance	9	4
Other industries	28	0
Total	654	578

Source: Obie G. Whichard, "U.S. Direct Investment Abroad in 1976," *Survey of Current Business*, August 1977.

TABLE 3.4

Sales by Majority-Owned Foreign Affiliates of U.S. Companies in Jamaica, 1975
($ million)

Sector	Total Sales	Local Sales	Export Sales to the United States	Export Sales to Other Countries
Mining and smelting	271	8	245	18
Petroleum	155	[52]*	0	103
Manufacturing	112	99	12	1
Trade	10	[10]*	0	0
Other industries	212	197	5	10
Total	760	366	262	132

*Figures in brackets were imputed from figures given in the remainder of the table.
Source: William K. Chung, "Sales by Majority-owned Foreign Affiliates of U.S. Companies, 1975," *Survey of Current Business*, February 1977.

to the world; export sales by these firms to the United States accounted for 87 percent of the total value of Jamaican exports to the United States.

The United States is now the most important trading partner for the Caribbean. It supplies the largest share of the value of the region's imports and provides a market for the major share of the region's exports. Table 3.5 shows that in 1974 over 45 percent of all Caribbean exports went to the United States. Exports from Jamaica and Trinidad to the United States accounted for 48 percent and 60 percent, respectively, of the value of their total exports.

TABLE 3.5

Percentage Distribution of Trade among Major Trading Partners, 1973–74

	Imports							
	Jamaica		Guyana		Trinidad and Tobago		Barbados	
Country	1973	1974	1973	1974	1973	1974	1973	1974
United States	38.6	35.3	24.2	25.7	16.2	10.6	21.1	19.3
United Kingdom	16.7	12.4	25.4	20.4	11.2	5.4	24.6	20.4
Canada	6.8	5.4	5.2	4.9	4.1	2.1	11.3	9.0
Venezuela	7.3	14.7	0.0	0.0	5.2	2.6	0.0	9.9
Commonwealth Caribbean	5.3	7.6	22.1	26.4	2.6	1.7	13.07	17.46
Saudi Arabia	0.0	0.0	0.0	0.0	23.5	35.5	0.0	0.0
Indonesia	0.0	0.0	0.0	0.0	9.6	18.0	0.0	0.0
Ecuador	0.0	0.0	0.0	0.0	6.7	6.7	0.0	0.0
	Domestic Exports							
United States	41.1	47.8	21.0	27.5	52.6	60.8	16.56	27.05
United Kingdom	23.1	15.7	29.5	20.8	4.7	2.2	33.23	15.52
Canada	5.1	4.5	5.0	5.2	1.6	2.4	5.55	5.58
Norway	10.6	10.7	0.0	0.0	0.0	0.0	0.0	0.0
Commonwealth Caribbean	6.2	4.4	15.7	11.3	11.9	8.1	27.97	22.16

Sources: Barbados: *Overseas Trade 1974* (Bridgetown: Statistical Service, 1975); Guyana: *Annual Account Relating to External Trade 1974* (Georgetown: Ministry of Economic Development, 1975); Jamaica: *External Trade, Annual Review 1974* (Kingston: Department of Statistics, 1975); Trinidad and Tobago: *Overseas Trade 1974* (Port-of-Spain: Central Statistical Office, 1976).

Trinidad's economy is dominated by its petroleum refining industry and the large share of imports from Saudi Arabia and Indonesia represents crude oil (as Table 3.4 indicates), most of which is refined in Trinidad and then exported to the United States. In the case of the smaller economies of Guyana and Barbados, the data for 1973–74 in Table 3.5 indicate that the United States and the United Kingdom share roughly the same proportion of imports and exports.

TRADE WITH THE UNITED STATES

Exports

Bauxite and Petroleum

The importance of the minerals industry in the Caribbean is illustrated by its contribution to gross domestic product. In 1976, petroleum contributed 48 percent of the GDP of Trinidad and Tobago and in 1975 bauxite and alumina contributed 10 percent and 14 percent, respectively, to the GDP of Jamaica and Guyana. The contribution of these industries to foreign exchange and to government revenues is even more significant than their percentage contribution to GDP indicates. In 1975, for example, petroleum exports accounted for 88 percent of Trinidad's total exports and contributed 66 percent to total government revenues; bauxite and alumina accounted for 64 percent of Jamaica's total exports and provided tax revenues amounting to some 32 percent of recurrent revenues.[*]

The United States imports about 90 percent of the bauxite it consumes, 35 percent of the alumina, and 1 percent of the aluminum metal.[2] In 1977, Jamaica and Guyana combined supplied 65 percent of the U.S. bauxite imports (56 percent for Jamaica and 9 percent for Guyana, respectively) (see Table 3.6). Altogether the Caribbean (including Haiti, Surinam, and the Dominican Republic) supplied approximately 90 percent of the U.S. imports. Table 3.7 shows that in 1977 Jamaica ranked second only to Australia as a world supplier of aluminum oxide to the United States and first among Caribbean suppliers.

Since the United States is the major market for Caribbean bauxite, the behavior of U.S. aluminum production directly affects the foreign exchange earnings of Caribbean producers. The results of regression analyses (given in Table 3.8) indicate that over the period 1955–73, a generally elastic relationship existed between U.S. aluminum production and the exports of bauxite and alumina from the Caribbean. For example, a 1 percent change in the value of aluminum production was accompanied by a 2.08 percent change in the value of Jamaica's bauxite and alumina exports.

---

[*]This does not include income and other taxes paid out of the income of bauxite industry workers.

As the major Commonwealth Caribbean producer of petroleum,[3] Trinidad's share of the U.S. petroleum market is small, despite the fact that 60 percent of its total petroleum exports goes to the United States. Between 1973 and 1977, there has been an almost fivefold increase in the value of U.S. petroleum imports from Trinidad and Tobago (from $346 million to $1,601 million). In addition, there has been a marked change in the composition of those imports. In 1973, fuel oil accounted for 63 percent of the value of U.S.

TABLE 3.6

U.S. Imports of Bauxite and Aluminum Oxide, 1977

Country	Thousand Long Tons	$ million (f.a.s.)[a]	Percent of Total Bauxite Imports	
			Quantity	Value
Calcined Bauxite (2833020)				
Guyana	215.9	21.6	1.61	5.9
Surinam	21.4	1.7	.16	.5
Other	.5	.5	0.0	.1
Total	237.8	23.8	1.77	6.5
Bauxite Except Calcined (2833040)				
Jamaica	7,325.3	204.8	54.7	56.5
Haiti	578.4	15.4	4.3	4.2
Dominican Republic	738.8	21.8	5.5	6.0
Guyana	373.6	8.5	2.8	2.3
Surinam	1,887.9	43.8	14.0	12.0
Greece	56.3	.4	.4	.1
Guinea	2,123.5	43.0	15.8	11.9
Sierra Leone	78.9	.9	.6	.2
Other	.0	.0	0.0	0.0
Grand total	13,400.5	362.4	100.0[b]	100.0[b]

[a]f.a.s. = free alongside ship.
[b]Due to rounding, figures may not add up to 100.0.
Source: U.S. Department of Commerce, *U.S. General Imports—Schedule A Commodity by Country*, FT 135 (Washington, D.C.: Government Printing Office, December 1977).

TABLE 3.7

U.S. Imports of Aluminum Hydroxide and Oxide, 1977
(Schedule A 5136540)

Country	Thousand Pounds	$ million (f.a.s.)	Percent of Total Aluminum Hydroxide and Oxide Imports	
			Quantity	Value
Canada	45,179.4	4.6	5.4	.9
Jamaica	1,385,598.7	106.9	16.7	20.9
Guyana	117,629.0	6.6	1.4	1.3
Surinam	841,938.6	47.0	10.1	9.2
United Kingdom	361.7	.3	0.0	0.0
Netherlands	234.2	.5	0.0	0.0
France	18,934.6	13.6	.2	2.6
West Germany	54,972.6	6.9	.6	1.3
Japan	114,572.8	6.8	1.3	1.3
Australia	5,710,544.0	318.1	68.8	62.2
Other	205.3	.06	0.0	0.0
Total	8,290,170.9	511.36	100.0*	100.0*

*Due to rounding, figures may not add up to 100.0.

Source: U.S. Department of Commerce, *U.S. General Imports—Schedule A Commodity by Country*, FT 135 (Washington, D.C.: Government Printing Office, December 1977).

petroleum imports from Trinidad, while crude petroleum accounted for 16 percent. In 1977 the share of crude oil imports rose sharply to 46 percent while fuel oil fell to 38 percent (see Table 3.9). Over the same period, Trinidad's share of total U.S. petroleum imports declined from 4.6 to 3.8 percent.

Sugar

Sugar is the principal agricultural export of the Caribbean and therefore a major earner of foreign exchange. In 1975, sugar exports accounted for 53.7 percent of the total domestic exports of Barbados. For Guyana, Jamaica, and Trinidad, the respective percentages were 49.7, 19.9, and 4.3 percent.

Traditionally, the United States has never been a major market for Commonwealth Caribbean sugar. Between 1954 and 1972, the share of Caribbean sugar exports to the United States fluctuated sharply, reaching a peak of 21 percent in 1961, shortly after the United States broke off diplomatic relations with Cuba. Between 1961 and 1972, the U.S. share fell to as low as 11 percent.[4] In 1977, Jamaica, Trinidad and Tobago, Guyana, and Barbados supplied less than 5 percent of the total U.S. sugar imports from the Caribbean and Latin America (see Table 3.10).

The year 1974 was an important one for the Caribbean sugar industry. Both the Commonwealth Sugar Agreement and the U.S. Sugar Act expired at the end of that year, the former being replaced by new agreements with the European Economic Community (EEC) under the Lomé Convention, and the quota system of the latter by the world market and new tariffs. Due to bad weather and other factors, sugar prices in 1974 reached their highest point in 50 years, providing substantial increases in foreign exchange for Caribbean producers. (By the end of 1975, prices had fallen sharply.)

The sugar industry in the Caribbean has been undergoing a process of rationalization. In Jamaica and Barbados, the number of factories has been reduced to eliminate inefficiency. New industrial technology in harvesting and in the sugar extraction process promises to increase production efficiency in the future. Jamaica has committed more sugar lands to production and the amount of sugar extracted per ton has increased since 1970.

These improvements notwithstanding, the industry faces a fundamental problem, illustrated by the Barbadian situation. Between 1968 and 1974, Barbados had to import labor from neighbouring islands to reap its sugar cane

TABLE 3.8

Elasticity of Bauxite and Alumina Exports with Respect to U.S. Aluminum Production

Country	Regression (elasticity) Coefficients	t-statistic	R^2
Jamaica (1955–73)			
Bauxite	2.04	8.34	.80
Alumina	2.34	14.37	.92
Bauxite and alumina	2.08	11.81	.89
Guyana (1961–73)			
Bauxite	2.12	11.51	.92
Alumina	1.02	3.52	.53
Bauxite and alumina	1.60	11.16	.91

Source: Computations are based on data in Tables D.3, D.4, and D.19.

TABLE 3.9

U.S. Imports of Petroleum from Trinidad and Tobago and the World, 1973 and 1977

Schedule A: Commodity Grouping	Total U.S. Imports 1973 Thousand Barrels	$ million (f.a.s.)*	1977 Thousand Barrels	$ million (f.a.s.)*	U.S. Imports from Trinidad 1973 Thousand Barrels	$ million (f.a.s.)*	1977 Thousand Barrels	$ million (f.a.s.)*
Crude Petroleum								
3310120	136,302.6	399.1	113,662.9	1,374.6	1,712.2	4.6	0.0	0.0
3310140	1,157,406.1	3,831.6	2,406,142.0	32,207.9	8,186.8	29.2	50,061.3	731.8
3310210	697.4	3.4	0.0	0.0	9.7	.1	0.0	0.0
3310220	2,406.0	30.9	0.0	0.0	473.8	1.3	0.0	0.0
3310230	86,562.2	289.0	0.0	0.0	5,597.1	18.5	0.0	0.0
3310240	6,781.2	26.7	0.0	0.0	118.7	1.1		
Total		4,580.7		33,207.5		54.8		
Fuel Oil								
3323020	35,240.5	86.2	2,686.7	36.5	911.6	2.2	449.6	6.3
3323040	152,060.1	629.5	46,768.0	705.3	10,815.0	37.6	5,928.5	84.1
3324020	447,263.8	1,276.0	358,220.2	4,501.5	28,372.6	75.4	25,777.5	323.8
3324040	99,916.2	411.1	49,261.7	685.9	25,341.9	101.6	13,287.6	191.1
Total		2,402.8		5,929.2		216.8		605.3

Gasoline and Motor Fuel								
3321000	18,929.9	149.0	23,592.8	377.1	1,365.1	9.9	5,206.7	89.8
Jet Fuel 3322020	69,539.8	297.8	22,501.8	349.1	12,275.7	60.3	4,753.1	73.3
Kerosene 3322040	1,077.5	6.9	846.7	13.3			201.3	3.2
Naphtha 3329920	11,095.0	46.5	65,177.4	952.5	2,076.8	4.1	6,141.3	93.5
Liquid Derivatives								
3329940	0.0	24.3	0.0	73.4	0.0	0.0	0.0	4.1
Grand Total		7,508.0		41,277.1		345.9		1,601.0

*The f.a.s. represents the transaction value of imports at the foreign port of exportation. It is based on the purchase price, that is, the actual transaction value, and generally includes all charges incurred in placing the merchandise alongside the carrier at the port of exportation in the country of exportation.

Source: U.S. Department of Commerce, Bureau of the Census, *U.S. Imports—General and Consumption, Schedule A Commodity by Country, Report* FT 135 (Washington, D.C.: Government Printing Office, December 1973 and December 1977).

because of the shortage of labor. In 1975 and 1976, local labor was induced to return to harvest the cane only because it was offered higher wages. If higher wages exist in other sectors of the economy, some workers would choose to be unemployed rather than reap cane. If the sugar industry is to pay higher wages, productivity must increase; to increase productivity, the industry must become increasingly capital-intensive. Political constraints operate to prevent many Caribbean countries from rushing headlong into new capital investments in the sugar industry. Such investments would displace labor, perpetuate the vulnerability of their economies to world market fluctuations, and force their

TABLE 3.10

U.S. Sugar Imports from Caribbean and Latin American Countries, 1977
(f.a.s.)

Country	$ million	Percent of Total
Columbia	2.6	.5
Salvador	23.4	4.1
Honduras	5.4	.9
Dominican Republic	169.9	29.8
Trinidad and Tobago	9.4	1.6
Peru	47.6	8.4
Bolivia	8.7	1.5
Brazil	88.2	15.5
Argentina	48.0	8.4
Barbados	8.2	1.4
Belize	6.2	1.0
Nicaragua	25.5	4.5
Panama	22.2	3.9
Jamaica	6.4	1.1
Guyana	3.1	.5
Ecuador	9.5	1.6
Guatemala	63.1	11.0
Costa Rica	18.3	3.2
Leeward and Windward Islands	3.6	.6
Total	569.3	100.0*

*Due to rounding, figures may not add up to 100.0.
Source: U.S. Department of Commerce, *U.S. General Imports, Schedule A Commodity by Country*, FT 135 (Washington, D.C.: Government Printing Office, December 1977).

governments to negotiate with foreign governments for protected markets. Given these problems, it is perhaps not surprising that several of the Caribbean countries, especially the smaller islands, view the development of a tourist industry as a viable alternative to sugar as an earner of foreign exchange. Tourism has already replaced sugar in importance in Barbados and that country's long-run strategy is to develop a strong manufacturing sector.

Wider access to markets for Caribbean agriculture and processed agricultural exports is the main feature of the convention signed in Lomé in February 1975 between the EEC and 46 African, Caribbean, and Pacific (ACP) states. The convention exempts ACP agricultural and processed agricultural products from customs duties and gives preference to ACP products over those from third countries. In addition to an EEC commitment to purchase approximately 1.4 million metric tons of ACP sugar at a guaranteed price, the Lomé Convention also provides for a mechanism to stabilize the export earnings of 12 basic products or groups of products. The inclusion of processed agricultural products provides an important stimulus to the development of manufacturing activities which utilize local agricultural raw materials in the ACP countries. This is of particular significance for the Caribbean sugar industry, which accounts for a large share of the value of manufactured exports.

Despite the Lomé Convention, the future of sugar in the Caribbean is the subject of intense debate. Much of the discussion centers around diversification into other groups. G. B. Hagelberg cites a wide variety of evidence to show that in spite of selected successful diversification programs, agricultural diversification in the Caribbean has not been generally successful because the export earnings per acre of sugar have been higher than that for alternative crops.[5] He is not convinced by the arguments of Caribbean economists who question the contribution of the sugar industry to the development of the Caribbean. Rather than abandoning sugar as Brewster and others[6] have suggested, Hagelberg argues that since no alternative tropical crop has yet been found that will employ large numbers of workers and extensive acreage with a productivity equal to that of sugar,

> the best development strategy would seem to be one that seeks diversification through rather than apart from sugar cane. While not neglecting the possibilities of improving productivity in other crops by research and more intensive application of modern farming practices, machinery, and chemicals, the aim would be to exploit sugar cane not only as a source of sugar for human consumption (or foreign exchange earnings from sugar exports) but also as a source of feed and fiber.[7]

Hagelberg brings out two important points regarding the character of the Caribbean sugar industry which prevent the Caribbean from benefiting fully from high market prices for sugar. One is the inability of the Caribbean to exploit marketing opportunities because of its limited productive capacity, and the other (related to the first) is that Caribbean exports have tended to fluctuate with current production in the absence of reserves.

While the English-speaking Caribbean has not been a major source of U.S. sugar imports, it has been a major source of sugar workers for the U.S. sugar industry. Over the past decade, the United States has imported 10,000 to 15,000 sugar workers annually under contract with Caribbean governments. There will be a further discussion of this in Chapter 6.

Manufactured Goods

Manufactured goods account for a relatively small share of total exports for all Caribbean countries. Yet in 1975 manufacturing's contribution to GDP was 16 percent for Jamaica, over 7 percent for Trinidad, 5 percent for Guyana, and roughly 11 percent for Barbados. Unlike the mining sector, U.S. direct investment in manufacturing in the Caribbean is oriented toward local sales. Thus access to the U.S. market does not enjoy the same ease as bauxite and alumina which are raw materials produced for the parent firms. The Generalized System of Preferences (GSP) provided for in the U.S. Trade Reform Act of 1974, and which took effect in January 1976, is designed to offer easier access to the U.S. market for manufactured products from developing countries. It allows duty-free entry into the U.S. market of a specified list of more than 2,700 products, imported directly from about 140 developing countries (and worth more than $2.5 billion in 1974 U.S. trade) for a period of seven years.[8] In order for a product to be eligible, the value-added in the developing country must be at least 35 percent of its value, except in those cases where the country is a member of a free trade association in which the local content from the association must be 50 percent. The law also excludes imports from any one country if the article exceeds $25 million or 50 percent of the total U.S. imports of that article. At this point the GSP has had little impact on the export of Caribbean manufactured goods to the United States.[9]

Tourism

Perhaps the most visible component of Caribbean trade with the United States is tourism, in spite of the fact that it is treated in the Caribbean balance-of-payments accounts as invisible trade. The figures in Table 3.11 indicate that of the four countries, tourism is more important for Jamaica and Barbados than for Trinidad and Tobago and Guyana. (Indeed, it is most important for Barbados and least so for Guyana.) The discussion here will accordingly focus on Barbados and Jamaica.

A look at the flow of tourists for the period 1971–75 (see Table 3.12) shows that the source of Barbadian tourists is far less concentrated than Jamaica's. In 1975, for example, Canada supplied the largest share of stopover tourists (those who stay one or more nights) to Barbados (34 percent), followed by the United States (24.7 percent), the United Kingdom (24.7), and the Commonwealth

Caribbean (17.1 percent). In that same year, the United States supplied 75.2 percent of the tourists going to Jamaica.

Between 1965 and 1974, the tourist industry in Jamaica and Barbados experienced a steady growth, both in terms of the number of stopover tourists and the volume of tourist expenditures (see Table 3.13). The number of stopover tourists visiting Jamaica grew from 189,000 to 433,000, and the volume of tourist spending rose from $55.6 million to $145.4 million.[10] Thus a 129 percent increase in the number of stopover tourists was accompanied by a 161 percent increase in their spending.

The figures for Barbados show an even greater increase in the level of tourist-industry activity. The number of stopover tourists in the same period moved from 68,400 to 231,000 (an increase of 239 percent); spending grew from $13 million to $70 million (an increase of 438 percent). Throughout the period, per capita tourist spending in Jamaica was consistently higher than that in Barbados.

Many factors affect the performance of the Caribbean tourist industry. Chief among them are economic conditions in the United States and Canada, the relative cost of air transportation, and the stability of social and political conditions in the host countries. All these variables have been in a state of flux in the 1970s. The United States and other developed Western countries have gone through a major recession cum inflation precipitated by the 1973 oil crisis; and fear of inflation has led them to pursue conservative monetary and fiscal policies

TABLE 3.11

Tourist Receipts as a Percentage of Exports of Goods and Services, 1970–75

Year	Jamaica	Trinidad and Tobago	Barbados	Guyana
1970	17.7	N.A.	34.3	2.2
1971	16.3	8.6	39.2	2.0
1972	21.3	8.2	47.0	1.9
1973	19.6	7.3	44.5	2.3
1974	13.3	4.6	45.0	0.4
1975	11.3	5.1	38.7	N.A.

Sources: Economic and Social Survey Jamaica 1970; 1975 (Kingston: The Government Printer, 1971, 1976); *Balance of Payments of Trinidad and Tobago* (Port-of-Spain: Central Statistical Office, 1975); *Balance of Payments of Barbados, 1973* (Bridgetown: Statistical Service, 1974); Guyana, *Annual Statistical Abstract, 1974* (Georgetown: Ministry of Economic Development, 1975); *Annual Statistical Digest* (Bridgetown: Central Bank of Barbados, 1975).

TABLE 3.12

Country of Origin of Stopover Tourists Visiting Jamaica and Barbados, 1971–75

Country	1971		1972		1973		1974		1975	
	Number	Percent	Number	Percent	Number	Percent	Number	Percent	Number	Percent
United States										
Jamaica	292,460	81.4	316,191	77.5	325,315	77.8	339,694	78.4	297,326	75.2
Barbados	68,487	36.2	75,525	35.9	74,779	33.6	66,237	28.7	14,894	24.7
Canada										
Jamaica	28,165	7.8	38,331	9.4	36,867	8.8	37,445	8.7	46,769	11.8
Barbados	53,690	28.3	61,918	29.4	68,639	30.9	77,246	33.4	75,517	34.0
United Kingdom										
Jamaica	9,234	2.6	16,860	4.1	17,737	4.2	17,201	4.0	15,987	4.0
Barbados	13,621	7.2	14,851	7.0	17,690	7.9	23,782	10.3	24,802	11.2
Commonwealth Caribbean										
Jamaica	8,716	2.4	13,745	3.4	15,129	3.6	14,110	3.3	11,030	2.8
Barbados	33,892	17.9	36,608	17.4	36,349	16.3	38,139	16.5	38,070	17.1

		%		%		%		%		%
Other										
Jamaica	20,739	5.8	22,679	5.6	23,209	5.6	24,537	5.6	24,697	6.2
Barbados	19,385	10.2	21,447	10.2	24,623	11.0	25,314	10.9	28,203	12.7
Total										
Jamaica	323,232	100.0	407,806	100.0	418,257	100.0	432,987	100.0	395,809	100.0
Barbados	189,075	100.0	210,349	100.0	222,080	100.0	230,718	100.0	221,486	100.0

Sources: *Annual Statistical Digest, 1975* (Bridgetown: Central Bank of Barbados, 1976); *Economic and Social Survey Jamaica 1975* (Kingston: Department of Statistics, 1976).

to restrain growth. This in turn has tended to moderate the growth of tourist spending. (See Appendix B for a more detailed analysis of the relationship between tourist spending and economic conditions in the United States.)

In Jamaica, the more than doubling of the volume of tourist trade between 1965 and 1974 led to overexpansion of industry capacity, in spite of the post-1974 slump in tourist activity. Hotel accommodations grew from 6,204 beds at the end of 1965 to 16,607 at the end of 1975—a 168 percent increase. Despite the growth of the number of stopover tourists in the late 1960s and early 1970s, hotel occupancy rates began a steady decline from a peak in 1969 of 62.1 percent to 30.4 percent in 1976. Thus, while the aggregate figures indicate an expanding industry, they are belied by the 50 percent reduction in occupancy rates. Indeed, the 30.4 percent occupancy rate in 1976 is far below the 55 percent the industry considers a break-even point. Many hotels have gone bankrupt and the government, desperate for foreign exchange, has taken steps to purchase them in

TABLE 3.13

Stopover Tourists and Tourist Expenditures for Jamaica and Barbados, 1964–75

	Jamaica		Barbados	
Year	Stopover Tourists[a] (thousands)	Tourist Expenditures[b] ($ million)	Stopover Tourists[a] (thousands)	Tourist Expenditures[b] ($ million)
1964	N.A.	37.4	57.6	12.8
1965	189.0	55.6	68.4	13.0
1966	228.1	67.2	77.1	14.5
1967	235.0	68.8	91.5	17.4
1968	258.4	87.8	115.7	19.7
1969	276.9	93.4	134.3	26.9
1970	359.1	95.5	156.4	28.4
1971	359.3	108.9	189.0	31.7
1972	407.8	129.4	210.3	42.6
1973	418.2	138.9	222.0	62.2
1974	432.9	145.4	230.7	69.9
1975	395.8	140.1	221.4	N.A.

[a]Does not include cruise passengers and members of the armed forces.

[b]The exchange rates used for conversion of Jamaican and Barbadian dollars into U.S. dollars are (J) $1.00 = (U.S.) $1.20 and (B) $1.00 = (U.S.) $0.50.

Sources: Economic and Social Survey Jamaica 1965–75 (Kingston: The Government Printer, 1966–76); *Economic Survey Barbados, 1968, 1971,* (Bridgetown: Economic Planning Unit, 1969, 1972); *Monthly Digest of Statistics Barbados 1976* (Bridgetown Statistical Service, 1976).

the hope that subsidizing a failing venture will continue to generate the foreign exchange that would otherwise be lost.

The absolute cost of air fares to the Caribbean has risen at a time when air fares within the United States and between the United States and Europe have been cut substantially due to competition among carriers. These factors have increased the relative cost of traveling to the Caribbean. To attract visitors, national tourist agencies in the region have resorted heavily to packaged tours which provide low-cost air transportation and hotel accommodations. Since tourists who take advantage of package deals tend to spend less, this development has effectively reduced per capita expenditures by visitors. The implication is that larger numbers of tourists attracted to Jamaica may not generate the expected employment—and the foreign exchange sought by the government in initially taking over the failing hotels.[11]

The volatile character of the demand for Caribbean tourism is illustrated by a factor which had a devastating effect on the industry: the widespread publicity given to the uncertain social and political conditions in Jamaica in 1976 and 1977. Travel agents in the United States and Canada deliberately directed large numbers of prospective visitors to other destinations at that time. Consequently, tourist activity declined sharply. Thus, dependence on the tourism industry as a source of foreign exchange may operate to restrain a country's foreign policy pursuits or even the pursuit of domestic policies that appear to reduce the influence of the foreign investor. There are no long-term contractual arrangements to supply tourist services; the industry operates on a season-by-season basis. One bad season for a small economy with a balance-of-payments problem can seriously curtail its ability to finance incremental imports.

The foreign-exchange benefits of the industry must always be weighed against social costs. The sharp decline in occupancy rates between 1969 and 1976 suggests that capital invested in the industry could have been more socially productive elsewhere. Part of this capital represented loans guaranteed by the local government (in the case of Jamaica); when some of these ventures failed, the government was left holding the proverbial bag.

Substantial economic rents must be collected from a beautiful natural environment without eventually endangering the source of those rents. Every country has an obligation to the welfare of its people to exploit these rents judiciously. Good planning and good management of planned projects can improve the value of these rents and thus the potential for enhancing the welfare and culture of the local people.

Imports

Food

Table 3.14 provides a measure of the growth of Caribbean external dependence on food supplies over the period 1965–76. Beginning in 1969, the four countries began to experience a deficit in their combined balance of trade in agriculture and food products. Throughout the entire period, Trinidad and Tobago had a deficit which reached a peak in 1973 and a low in 1975. Guyana, on the other hand, has experienced a surplus throughout the period. Both Jamaica and Barbados began to suffer deficits in 1969. Favorable sugar prices in 1975 provided a temporary break in the rising regional deficit, producing a surplus for the region as a whole as well as for Jamaica and Barbados. The Trinidad and Tobago deficit was sharply reduced while Guyana increased its surplus.

The long-run trend is clearly one of increasing dependence on external sources of food. Domestic supply has not been able to keep pace with demand. But perhaps even more importantly, the growth of income and the accompanying change in the structure of demand has increased the propensity to import foreign foods. Thus as income grows, the share of imported foods in the total supply grows, placing a greater claim on more foreign exchange. One may conclude that the problem of food in the Caribbean is as much a demand problem as it is one of supply. Weeks has argued that the demand problem is

TABLE 3.14

Imports of Agricultural and Food Products* as a Percentage of Exports, 1965–76

Year	Jamaica	Trinidad and Tobago	Guyana	Barbados	Total
1965	75.0	158.6	37.9	78.9	80.4
1966	77.5	171.6	38.5	80.8	82.7
1967	86.2	159.3	24.9	72.0	81.3
1968	97.1	123.2	34.1	83.0	82.3
1969	101.7	144.7	35.6	110.7	118.4
1970	122.8	145.4	36.2	129.2	102.6
1971	133.6	164.8	34.7	148.7	109.4
1972	143.3	157.8	30.4	181.3	113.3
1973	152.3	286.8	48.6	162.0	142.4
1974	144.0	181.8	22.6	102.0	98.4
1975	94.8	130.0	20.1	66.7	72.2
1976	153.2	235.0	32.7	124.9	123.8

*Sections 0, 1, and 4 of Standard Industrial Trade Classification.

Source: Based on data from the Caribbean Food and Nutrition Institute, Kingston, Jamaica, 1977.

related to the maldistribution of income which "generates a structure of demand inconsistent with the resource endowments of poor countries." [12] To the extent that the problem is one of local supply, it springs from the neglect of agriculture in the development strategies of the 1960s. The emphasis then on industrial development of urban areas had the effect of upsetting the rural-urban balance by attracting a disproportionate share of the population to urban areas. This meant the allocation of an increasing share of public expenditures to providing urban services at the expense of agricultural development.

The extent of Caribbean dependence on food imports is also reflected in Table 3.15, which shows that food imports range from 6.6 percent of total imports in Trinidad and Tobago to 22.5 percent in Barbados. Table 3.16 shows that the United States supplied well over a third of the food imports of Jamaica, Guyana, and Trinidad and Tobago. Principal among the foods imported are grain and grain flour (Standard International Trade Classification [SITC] groups 041, 044, and 046). In 1974, all the countries (with the exception of Barbados) imported anywhere from 77 to 92 percent of their grain and grain flour from the United States (see Table 3.17).

The high dependence of the Caribbean on imported food may be illustrated by using Jamaica, the largest of the four economies, as an example. In 1973, its imports of cereal and cereal preparations, meat and meat preparations, and fish and fish preparations were, respectively, 30.2 percent, 21.6 percent, and 17.2 percent of total food imports. Together these items accounted for 34 percent of all consumer goods imports. Even more striking is the fact that these three categories of food imports represented 45.6 percent of the value of the GDP in Jamaica's agricultural sector.

The total GDP of the food production for domestic consumption in 1973 was (J) $144.19 million. This includes the categories of domestic agriculture, livestock and hunting, fishing, and manufactured food.* In that same year, personal consumption expenditures for food alone were (J) $374.8 million, representing 30.3 percent of total personal consumption expenditures.† Even if we make an allowance for the domestic consumption of sugar and molasses, the gap between domestic food production and domestic food consumption is large. When we add the (J) $84 million of food imports to the food GDP, we get approximately (J) $222 million. The difference between this figure and the personal expenditures for food represents the mark-up of (J) $152 million by the wholesale and retail sectors. [13]

---

*Sugar, rum, and molasses are excluded because these products are primarily for export. If nonalcoholic beverages were included, the figure would be (J) $148.1 million.

†In 1974, food and beverages represented 21.4 percent of personal consumption expenditure. When beverages are added to food expenditures for Jamaica, they both account for 38 percent of total personal consumption expenditures.

TABLE 3.15

Percentage Distribution of Trade by SITC Classification, 1974

Item	Jamaica	Guyana	Trinidad and Tobago	Barbados
	Imports			
0 Food	20.5	12.7	6.6	22.5
1 Beverages and tobacco	0.7	0.5	0.3	1.8
2 Crude materials	3.3	1.0	0.6	2.8
3 Mineral fuels	20.3	18.2	71.9	15.8
4 Animal and vegetable oils	1.3	2.1	0.6	1.7
5 Chemicals	9.5	11.8	3.0	8.3
6 Manufactured articles	21.2	24.5	8.2	19.0
7 Machinery and transport equipment	16.6	21.5	6.3	14.3
8 Miscellaneous manufacturing	5.4	6.7	2.0	10.1
9 Miscellaneous transactions and commodities	0.2	0.4	0.1	3.?

Exports

0 Food	16.60	58.80	3.80	41.90
1 Beverages and tobacco	2.60	2.60	.30	4.10
2 Crude materials	72.80	34.30	.20	.90
3 Mineral fuels	1.40	.03	90.20	20.90
4 Animal and vegetable oils	.03	0.0	0.0	.01
5 Chemicals	1.50	.69	3.30	4.70
6 Manufactured articles	1.70	1.10	.60	4.60
7 Machinery and transport equipment	1.50	.30	.40	7.10
8 Miscellaneous manufacturing	1.50	1.30	.80	14.40
9 Miscellaneous transactions and commodities	.05	.50	0.0	.90

Sources: Barbados: *Overseas Trade 1974* (Bridgetown: Statistical Service, 1975); Guyana: *Annual Account Relating to External Trade 1974* (Georgetown: Ministry of Economic Development, 1975); Jamaica: *External Trade, Annual Review 1974* (Kingston: Department of Statistics, 1975); Trinidad and Tobago: *Overseas Trade 1974* (Port-of-Spain: Central Statistical Office, 1976).

TABLE 3.16

Share of Trade by Sections of SITC with the United States 1974

Item	Jamaica	Guyana	Trinidad and Tobago	Barbados
	Imports			
0 Food	40.60	42.50	36.20	17.50
1 Beverages and tobacco	42.20	13.30	16.30	9.40
2 Crude materials	38.70	52.50	18.30	14.10
3 Mineral fuels	4.20	.40	.08	1.50
4 Animal and vegetable oils	70.30	25.50	51.70	2.90
5 Chemicals	56.30	30.20	31.80	14.10
6 Manufactured articles	40.70	18.50	29.30	19.30
7 Machinery and transport equipment	44.40	39.90	57.70	44.20
8 Miscellaneous manufacturing	37.40	31.80	27.80	27.70
9 Miscellaneous transactions and commodities	7.00	25.20	24.20	15.50

	Exports			
0 Food	33.90	31.10	23.00	38.70
1 Beverages and tobacco	28.20	.04	12.30	4.40
2 Crude materials	52.50	25.70	4.20	.08
3 Mineral fuels	2.20	0.0	64.50	1.00
4 Animal and vegetable oils	10.80	0.0	0.0	0.0
5 Chemicals	8.00	0.70	24.00	1.00
6 Manufactured Articles	26.60	16.10	.08	8.20
7 Machinery and transport equipment	20.40	21.20	.50	65.20
8 Miscellaneous manufacturing	45.50	6.80	5.20	34.90
9 Miscellaneous transactions and commodities	66.10	16.20	17.50	20.20

*Includes reexports.

Sources: Barbados: *Overseas Trade 1974* (Bridgetown: Statistical Service, 1975); Guyana: *Annual Account Relating to External Trade 1974* (Georgetown: Ministry of Economic Development, 1975); Jamaica: *External Trade, Annual Review 1974* (Kingston: Department of Statistics, 1975); Trinidad and Tobago: *Overseas Trade 1974* (Port-of-Spain: Central Statistical Office, 1976).

Jamaica imported 52.2 million pounds of meat and meat preparations in 1974 to supplement the 89 million pounds it produced. Fifty-four percent—28.1 million pounds—of all imported meat and meat products came from the United States. In that same year, Jamaica imported 34.4 million pounds of fish and fish preparations to supplement its production of 36 million pounds. Of the total fish imports, the United States provided only 828,000 pounds, or 2.4 percent; the major suppliers were the United Kingdom, Spain, Canada, Japan, and the Netherlands. The two most important fish imports are dried codfish and salted mackerel in brine.

As we indicated earlier, cereal and cereal preparations constituted the largest single category of food imports. The three most important items under this category are wheat, rice, and maize (corn). The Caribbean is almost totally dependent on the United States for wheat and corn. Of the total of 894 million pounds of wheat, wheat flour, maize, and maize flour imported by the four countries in 1974, 723.6 million pounds (81 percent) came from the United States (see Table 3.17). The other important grain—rice—is imported largely from Guyana by Jamaica, Trinidad, and Barbados.

In summary, in two of the principal areas of food imports—meat and meat preparations and cereal and cereal preparations—the United States is the principal supplier. Climate, technology, capital, and vast agricultural lands

TABLE 3.17

Import of Grain (Wheat and Maize) and Grain Flour, 1974 (SITC Groups 041, 044, and 046)

| | | United States | |
Country	Total (million pounds)	Pounds (million)	Percentage of Total
Jamaica	384.9	295.7	76.8
Guyana	114.6	111.4	97.2
Trinidad and Tobago	340.3*	312.6	91.8
Barbados	54.3	3.9	7.1
Total	894.1	723.6	

*North America only.

Sources: Barbados; *Overseas Trade 1974* (Bridgetown: Statistical Service, 1975); Guyana: *Annual Account Relating to External Trade 1974* (Georgetown: Ministry of Economic Development, 1975); Jamaica: *External Trade, Annual Review 1974* (Kingston: Department of Statistics, 1975); Trinidad and Tobago: *Overseas Trade 1974* (Port-of-Spain: Central Statistical Office, 1976).

have combined to make the United States the world's most efficient producer of food. This combination of factors cannot be replicated in the countries of the Caribbean. Unless local or regional food sources are developed in the future to satisfy local and regional tastes and preferences for food, the United States is likely to remain the major source of Caribbean imported meat and grain. [14]

Studies of the prospect of rising food deficits in the developing countries by the U.S. Department of Agriculture (USDA) and the United Nations Food and Agricultural Organization (FAO) offer little comfort to the Caribbean:

> The FAO assessment concludes that on present trends, net grain imports by developing countries will rise from the 16 million ton annual average in 1969–71 to 85 million tons by 1985. If grain exporting developing countries such as Argentina and Thailand are excluded the projected deficit rises to around 100 million tons. The USDA study also projects sharply higher grain imports by the developing market economies, ranging between 48 and 72 million tons, except under the assumption of an acceleration in the use of fertilizer and other imports in the less developed countries. [15]

While the studies agree that the grain demanded by the developing countries can be met by the expansion of production in the United States, it is recognized that these imports by the developing countries "would place a heavy burden on the ability of the less developed countries to earn foreign exchange." [16]

The reduction and eventual elimination of the food deficit in the Caribbean requires a regional approach. A program called the Regional Food Plan is being developed jointly by Jamaica, Trinidad and Tobago, Guyana, Barbados, Belize, and the smaller Caribbean islands. The Caribbean Food Corporation was established in 1976 with a total share capital of (TT) $800 million to administer the Food Plan. It is expected that when the plan is fully developed in ten years, it will produce annually 574 pounds of milk, 51 million pounds of beef, 42 million pounds of mutton and lamb, 77 million chickens, 33.5 million pounds of soya beans, 2 million pounds of red kidney beans, and 2 million pounds of black-eyed peas. [17]

Machinery and Equipment

As a category, machinery and transport equipment represents a rough measure of capital goods imports, as well as the inflow of industrial technology embodied in these imports. Trade figures show that Caribbean countries import most of their machinery and transport equipment from the United States, underscoring the importance of the United States in the industrializaton of the Caribbean. However, much of this inflow goes directly to U.S. industrial operations in the region. This fact suggests that the importance of this category of imports in the balance of trade of the Caribbean reflects more the U.S. presence than the overall industrial development of the region. The share of this category in the total value of imports has ranged from 63 percent in Trinidad and Tobago to 21.5 percent in Guyana. For each country, over 40 percent of imports under this category came from the United States.

Because the modern U.S. industrial operations in the region are typically built to accept the advanced technology embodied in the capital goods imported from the United States, the transfer of embodied industrial technology tends to benefit the giant corporations more than the small locally owned operations. The transfer of technology embodied in capital equipment frequently dictates the adoption of managerial and operational techniques which more closely resemble those used in the country from which the embodied technology originates. This usually means massive investment outlays beyond what was originally intended in the developing areas. A local power company, for example, wishing to replace a worn-out piece of equipment may find that such equipment is no longer available and that units which are available have embodied in them technology not compatible with the rest of the company's operations. The company may therefore be forced to make a larger investment than it had planned in order to replace serviceable units to keep the plant operational.

Much has been discussed in the literature in recent years about choosing appropriate technology by developing countries. The choice for many is determined by what is available, however, and what is available is determined by the producers of technology. The real goal of the transfer of technology to developing countries should be to increase their ability to choose a mix of technology which is appropriate for their individual situations. To do so, they must themselves become producers of some technology, because as purely consumers of foreign technology with its built-in obsolescence, they are forced into continual dependence upon metropolitan producers for advancement.

TRADE WITH THE PERIPHERY

One of the most interesting features of the structure of Caribbean trade is that in addition to the region being traditionally a major exporter of crude (primary) materials, it has become a major importer of crude materials. For Jamaica, Guyana, and Trinidad, raw materials and intermediate goods averaged over 50 percent of imports in 1974. This, of course, is the result of the development of a number of import substitution industries. Much of the crude materials imported include crude food imports such as wheat and other grain which come largely from the United States. However, in recent years a significant share of crude materials imported by the Caribbean comes from the developing countries (the so-called periphery). In fact, it is reasonable to say that the structure of Caribbean trade with the periphery has been dominated by the import of primary materials. Thus we have a situation in which the simple center-periphery relationship which has previously provided the basic analytical framework for dependence arguments must be modified to accommodate a new dimension of dependence relationship, that is, dependence on the periphery itself.

The reported increase in the polarization between the center and the periphery since World War II has been characterized by the growth of the share of world trade among center countries and a general decline in the share of world trade among peripheral countries, with the exception of Latin America which has made some progress toward regional integration. This exception may also apply to the Commonwealth Caribbean which has made progress toward regional economic integration in the 1970s.

Jamaica's imports from CARICOM and Latin American countries, for example, grew from 8.4 percent of total imports in 1969 to 25 percent in 1975. This sharp increase is due primarily to oil imports, especially from Venezuela at substantially higher prices created by the oil crisis of 1973. The magnitude of the impact of the oil crisis on Jamaica's balance of payments is reflected in the relationship between its balance of trade with CARICOM and Latin America and the overall balance-of-trade deficit. In 1974 its balance-of-trade deficit with CARICOM and Latin America was 94 percent of the overall deficit compared to 13.3 percent in 1970 (see Table 3.18).

When the balance-of-trade deficit with CARICOM/Latin America is compared with the balance-of-trade deficit with the United States for 1974, Jamaica's trade position with the United States was relatively stronger. In fact, in 1973 there was a surplus of $7.7 million with the United States.

TRADE AND DEPENDENCE—AN ASSESSMENT

It is clear that the Caribbean has a high degree of trade dependence on the United States, but trade dependence does not of itself mean economic dependence, as small European countries such as the Netherlands and Belgium illustrate. The nature of economic dependence must be found in the structure of a country's economy. The dependent structure of the Caribbean economy is reflected in the overwhelming dominance of raw materials and semiprocessed goods in its trade—and little or no power to influence world market prices.

For some exports, no market transaction takes place. Bauxite shipped to the parent firm abroad is an intraindustry transaction governed by transfer pricing.[18] The value of the exports of bauxite to the parent firm is arbitrarily determined by that firm in a way that permits it to minimize its tax liability and to maximize its after-tax earnings. Royalties, licensing fees for parent-firm technology, and interest charges on loans from the parent firm are all determined by the parent firm. These payments may be deliberately inflated to increase the subsidiary's cost of production and thus reduce tax liability. The point of all this is that although a small developing country may be a major supplier of a vital raw material to companies in the United States, that small country has no power over prices.

TABLE 3.18

Jamaica's Trade with CARICOM and Latin America, 1969–75
(J $ million)

Item	1969	1970	1971	1972	1973	1974	1975
Imports	30.7	34.2	46.7	63.5	92.2	217.8	254.6
Exports	11.2	13.5	16.7	21.2	29.0	42.6	43.6
Balance of trade with CARICOM/L.A.	− 19.5	− 20.7	− 30.0	− 42.3	− 63.2	− 175.2	− 211.0
Balance of trade with the U.S.	− 39.6	− 43.9	− 54.5	− 53.9	− 97.5	+ 7.7	− 111.3
Imports from CARICOM/L.A. as percentage of total imports	8.4	7.8	10.1	12.8	15.0	25.5	24.9
Exports to CARICOM/L.A. as percent of total exports	3.9	4.7	5.8	7.0	8.1	6.4	6.1
Balance of trade with CARICOM/L.A. as percent of total balance on visible trade	16.3	13.3	17.0	21.9	25.3	93.9	68.3

Source: External Trade, Annual Review 1974, 1976 (Kingston: Department of Statistics, 1975, 1977).

This raises an important semantic confusion arising from the assertion so frequently heard that the United States is dependent upon the Third World for a wide range of vital raw materials. If dependence is interpreted to mean simply that the United States imports most of a particular raw material from a particular country, then the assertion is obviously true for such raw materials as manganese, cobalt, chromium, bauxite, and platinum. But the real meaning of dependence goes beyond the percentages exported to or imported from a particular country to include the decision-making mechanism which governs the production and marketing of these products. Quite often this decision-making mechanism is dominated by U.S. firms whose vast commitment of capital and technology has been predicated on the long-run stability of supply of raw materials.

The thrust of Third World economic policies over the past decade is to break the traditional link between metropolitan decision making and the export of vital raw material to the metropole. In other words, the objective is to replace the foreign decision makers with local decision makers who represent the local national interest. This drive to localize decision making is part of a larger quest for a new international economic order. Of course, the localization of decision making alone will not effectively redistribute economic power for the producers of raw materials. If local linkages are not developed to provide greater marketing flexibility, the fortunes of the local producers will continue to be determined by the demand of one or more of the metropolitan countries. This structural problem is also present in the petroleum industry and, in a peculiar way, in tourism as well. Both have traditionally been dominated by U.S. capital, and their consumers have been overwhelmingly North American.

Thus, as we have seen, one of the chief characteristics of Caribbean dependence on the metropole in general, and on the United States in particular, is that Caribbean industries tend to be more integrated with the metropolitan economies than with the local ones in which they are based. This situation is a major obstacle to the development of regional economic integration.

NOTES

1. Statement by Abelardo Valdez, Assistant Administrator for Latin America, Agency for International Development, before the Subcommittee on Inter-American Affairs, House International Relations Committee, June 28, 1977, p. 2.

2. Council on International Economic Policy, *Special Report: Critical Imported Materials* (Washington, D. C.: Government Printing Office, 1974), p. A–2.

3. The Trinidad economy is dominated by its oil industry and the oil industry is dominated by Texaco, the U.S. multinational oil company. Rothenberg and Wishner date the growth of the U. S. market for Trinidad oil back to 1959 when Texaco acquired Paragon Oil Company. As a result of this acquisition, "which for the first time allowed the company to engage directly in the fuel oil business in the large East Coast market, Texaco Trinidad's products began to redirect toward the U.S. market." Jane Rothenberg and Amy Wishner, "Focus on Trinidad," *NACLA's Latin America & Empire Report* 10 (1976): 17.

4. G. B. Hagelberg, *The Caribbean Sugar Industries: Constraints and Opportunities* (New Haven, Conn.: Yale University Antilles Research Program, 1974), p. 115.

5. Ibid., pp. 12–20.

6. Norman Girvan and Owen Jefferson, eds., *Readings in the Political Economy of the Caribbean* (Kingston: New World Group, 1971), pp. 37–76.

7. Hagelberg, op. cit., p. 19.

8. *International Economic Report of the President* (Washington, D. C.: Government Printing Office, 1977), p. 47.

9. Donald Baer provides an assessment of the first year impact of the GSP on the export of manufactured goods by Caribbean Basin countries to the United States:

> When both Basin sugar trade and Mexican trade are excluded from the GSP aggregations, the Basin's utilization of GSP becomes relatively negligible. In 1976, only about $200 million in potentially eligible goods other than sugar were imported into the U.S. from Basin economies other than Mexico. Of these goods, $86 million actually entered under GSP (43 percent), $31 million (16 percent) were excluded because of competitive need limitations, and $83 million (41 percent) did not or could not avail themselves of potential GSP eligibility.

Donald Baer, "U.S.-Basin Imports: Structure and the GSP," *Caribbean Basin Economic Survey* 3 (December 1977), p. 5.

10. No data is available on the number of Caribbean emigrants who return as tourists. However, definitions of broad groups of departing passengers (based upon their reason for travel) provided in the Jamaican government publication, *Demographic Statistics*, offer a clue. The figures show that for 1976, 56,378 departing passengers were listed under the heading, "To Reside." These passengers include "all Jamaicans who give a foreign home address or who are intending to take up residence abroad when leaving Jamaica." Jamaica, *Demographic Statistics* (Kingston: Department of Statistics, 1976).

By deducting from this figure the permanent migration to the United States, the United Kingdom, and Canada for that year (17,188), the balance (39,190) should provide a rough estimate of the number of Jamaicans who have returned as tourists. This latter figure represents 12 percent of the total number of stopover tourists for that year. Whether or not these Jamaican tourists are included in the number of stopover tourists is hard to say. The rather strange definition of a tourist used in the publication *Demographic Statistics* is: "All persons entering Jamaica from the U.S.A. and Canada who are not using their passports." (p. 99) Since most Jamaicans use their passports, especially those who are not yet U.S. or Canadian citizens, they would be excluded from this category. If they are in fact excluded, the number of stopover tourists which appears in published data understates the actual volume of tourist activity.

The growing importance of expatriate Jamaicans to the Jamaican tourist industry is recognized by the Jamaican government. In 1975, the then Deputy Prime Minister David Core visited Jamaican organizations in New York and Connecticut and emphasized that the tourist industry

> would have been in very bad shape this year, but for the support given by Jamaican nationals who returned home for vacation. The [Deputy Prime] Minister emphasized that those Jamaican organizations in New York and other states which were organizing group tours to Jamaica and using Air Jamaica as the carrier were by their efforts making substantial contributions to the Jamaican economy.

Jamaica Weekly Gleaner (NA), September 30, 1975, p. 2.

11. The *Jamaica Weekly Gleaner (NA)* has speculated editorially that subsidized package tours may be responsible for the industry's poor financial performance in the first three months of 1978—a period in which the number of tourists increased significantly. "Tourist Gold or Glitter?," *Jamaica Weekly Gleaner (NA)*, April 24, 1978, p. 13.

12. John Weeks, "Employment, Growth, and Foreign Domination in Underdeveloped Countries," A Warner Modular Publication Reprint from the *Review of Radical Political Economics* 4 (1972): R26–9.

13. Carl Stone argues that "the multiplicity of functionaries in the very complex distribution chain . . . simply adds to overhead costs and total mark-up margin." Carl Stone, "Prices and Markups," in *Essays on Power and Change in Jamaica*, eds. Carl Stone and Aggrey Brown (Kingston: Jamaica Publishing House, 1977), p. 143.

14. The tastes and preferences of Caribbean peoples for certain kinds of food contribute substantially to the large food import bill of the region. A few examples from Philip Sherlock's *This is Jamaica—An Informal Guide* (London: Hodder and Stoughton, 1968) are illustrative: "The most loved Jamaican dish is ackee and salt fish. What better proof of a divine ordering of human affairs is there, ask Jamaicans, than the fact that the ackee journeyed from West Africa in the slave ships to meet in Jamaica the salted cod that came south from the New England and Nova Scotia fisheries" (p. 30). In 1974, the import bill for that salted cod, which came largely from Spain, was (J) $4.9 million, or nearly 5 percent of the value of total food imports.

"Another national dish that sets the mouth of every exiled Jamaican watering is rice and peas" (pp. 30–31). Most of the rice consumed domestically is imported, with well over 50 percent coming from Guyana. The import bill for rice in 1974 was (J) $22.3 million, or approximately 20 percent of the total food import bill.

The taste for wheat products also contributed to the large food import bill. Total wheat imports (most of which came from the United States) in 1974 were (J) $9.5 million or 85 percent of the total import bill.

A third national dish is curried goat. In 1974 the import bill for imported goat meat, largely from India, was (J) $1.17 million.

15. Fred A. Sanderson, "Export Opportunities for Agricultural Products: Implications for US Agricultural and Trade Policies," *Columbia Journal of World Business* 10 (1977): 17.

16. Ibid.

17. Trinidad and Tobago, *Review of the Economy 1976* (Port-of-Spain: C.S.O. Printing Unit, 1976).

18. Rothenberg and Wishner (op. cit., p. 17) describe the method used by Texaco—the largest U.S. multinational corporation in Trinidad and Tobago—to reduce its tax liability to the host country.

> Texaco computes its refinery costs either at no profit or at a loss. Seventy-five percent of the crude that flows through Texaco's Trinidad refinery is imported from Texaco subsidiaries at prices pre-determined by the company. While the value-added through refining is considerable, Texaco Trinidad's revenues are not based on this differential but on a refining fee. As the fee barely covers the cost of processing, the company's Trinidad subsidiary ostensibly does not make a penny and who ever heard of taxing a company on money it did not make? A figure for government tax revenues from oil refining is not available. But it is instructive to notice that, in spite of the massive investment in refining during the period 1964–66, for example, a whopping 79 percent of total government revenues from the industry came from crude production alone.

They further point out (p. 20) that "in refining, not only did transfer pricing preclude the possibility of refining generating any revenues for the government . . . but foreign companies were also permitted to deduct so-called losses on refinery runs from profits on crude production."

4

Dependence and Economic Stability

For a small open developing economy, dependence essentially means being in the position of a price-taker. Such an economy is therefore vulnerable to fluctuations in the prices of externally traded goods. When these economies depend largely on the export of primary commodities, these fluctuations are particularly pronounced and are readily transmitted to domestic prices and income. Thus the problem of development for a small open developing country is also a problem of economic stability. When domestic prices are stable, the gains from the growth of output and trade can be better transmitted to the majority of the population to improve their well-being.

In order to set the stage for a discussion of exchange-rate policy and its implications for domestic price changes, this chapter will begin with a brief look at selected policy models. It will then focus on the roles of fiscal policy, monetary policy, and price controls as instruments of economic stabilization in the Caribbean context. The final section of the chapter underscores the policy dilemmas facing the small open developing Caribbean economies.

A THEORETICAL FRAMEWORK

The essential argument set forth here holds that monetary policy in the Caribbean setting of small open developing economies with fixed exchange rates plays a subservient role: it merely accommodates changes in the balance of payments and fiscal policy. Thus in contrast to the quantity theory of money, which posits the direction of causation from the money supply to prices, the ensuing discussion looks at the flow of causation in the opposite direction. This ordering of policy influence bears some resemblance to that of Hansen's model of an extremely open economy.[1] It is a purely recessive model; that is, in the hierarchy of policy instruments, the flow of causation is in one direction—from the most powerful policy instrument downwards, and not the other way around.

Thus in Bent Hansen's schematic ordering, "if a certain parameter appears for the first time in connection with variables of a certain order, this parameter can influence variables in this subset and in groups of a higher order, but never variables belonging to the subset of a lower order."[2] In Hansen's scheme, the lower the order, the more powerful the policy instrument. As the following schema shows, exchange policy is the most powerful, and credit policy the least powerful. All three variables—consumer price level, employment, and the balance of trade—are influenced by exchange-rate policy; fiscal and wage policy have influence over the employment and balance-of-trade variables; and credit policy has influence only over the balance-of-trade variable.

	Exchange Policy	Fiscal Policy and Wage Policy	Credit Policy
	Consumer Goods Price Level		
Spheres of Influence	Employment	Employment	
	Balance of Trade	Balance of Trade	Balance of Trade

It is clear from this ordering that fiscal and credit policies do not affect domestic prices. Changes in taxes, public expenditures, and the money stock are merely adjustments to domestic price changes generated by exchange-rate policy. The conclusion which flows from the Hansen model is that "in the extremely open economy, exchange policy must protect the value of money, (indirect) fiscal and wage policy must protect employment, and monetary and (direct) fiscal policy must protect the balance of payments."[3]

Despite the fact that the policy problem in the Hansen model is, as he himself puts it, "greatly simplified,"[4] it nevertheless has some relevance for the Caribbean, where monetary policy is subordinated to fiscal policy and where both are subordinated to exchange rate and tariff policies.[5]

A theoretical framework provided by R. A. Mundell is also a useful background against which to examine the problem of dependence and economic stability in the small open Caribbean economies.[6] Under conditions which require the central bank to intervene to maintain a fixed exchange rate, the expansionary effect of fiscal policy can be sustained in a small open economy. This would basically occur as a result of a series of adjustments initiated by an expansionary fiscal policy (deficit financing). Under the assumption that there is no domestic monetary action by the monetary authorities, the resulting increase in national income would increase the demand for money. With the domestic money supply fixed, interest rates would rise. But since the small open economy cannot influence interest rates in the international capital market, short-term capital would flow in to restore interest rates to their original level. The inflow of short-term capital would improve the balance of payments and thus cause the exchange rate to rise. Since the model assumes that the central bank is charged with keeping the exchange rate fixed, the central bank must sell its own currency (buy foreign exchange) to prevent the exchange rate from fluctuating. In the process of keeping the exchange rate fixed, the central bank has increased the supply of the domestic currency, thus permitting the increased demand for money to be met and the initial expansion of national income to be sustained. Thus, according to the Mundell model with its restrictive assumptions, the key to the effectiveness of expansionary fiscal policy under the conditions of a fixed exchange rate is an accompanying expansion of the money supply as a result of exchange-rate policy. Monetary policy, on the other hand, is shown to be ineffective under a fixed exchange-rate regime because an initial expansion of the money supply through open market operations is offset by the sale of foreign exchange (purchase of domestic currency) to maintain a fixed exchange rate.

One important assumption underlying this model is that domestic output is elastic and the price level constant. Thus the whole question of inflation is ignored. As Martin Prachowny observes, Mundell's "assumption of infinitely elastic supply of output seems to be relevant only to an economy suffering from a severe case of depression and not to the contemporary scene."[7]

June Flanders and Elahanan Helpman have made important modifications to the Mundell model. They have introduced assumptions of price flexibility and price rigidity in an effort to examine the impact of external and internal disturbances on domestic prices under regimes of fixed and flexible exchange rates. Under the assumption of flexible domestic prices, a flexible exchange-rate system will provide greater stability of domestic prices than will fixed exchange rates when external disturbances occur in the form of changes in the world prices of traded goods. This conclusion, they argue, is independent of the size of the traded goods sector and the degree of openness. Under a flexible exchange-rate system,

> a change in prices abroad will result in a change in the exchange rate that keeps the domestic price of the tradeable good constant; all real values will be constant, and so will be all nominal values in terms of local currency. The exchange rate fluctuations form a mirror image of changes in world prices.[8]

Under conditions of rigid domestic prices, a flexible exchange regime is also shown to be superior to a fixed exchange regime for the reason that

> equi-proportional changes in foreign prices affect only the exchange rate. Prices abroad rise and the price of foreign exchange falls as required to offset the rise. The domestic price level of traded goods is unchanged. Neither relative prices, nor the domestic price level, nor the non-traded good, has been affected. The economy has truly insulated itself from foreign disturbances in

this case, since the flexibility in the exchange rate serves as a substitute for flexibility in the domestic price of the non-traded goods.[9]

Flanders and Helpman conclude that

> the flexible rate regime implies full employment, whereas with fixed exchange rates, full employment may be possible only at the cost of a deficit in the balance of payments or a highly strained domestic "fiscal" policy. Even when full employment is maintainable with fixed exchange rates, in this case, the solution is second- not first-hand.[10]

With regard to the pegging of a small country's currency to that of a larger country, Flanders and Helpman argue that "since flexible rates are superior to fixed, they are also superior to a regime of pegging to a single large country."[11]

It is not easy to make the jump from any of the above models to the real situation of the Caribbean, or to that of any country for that matter, since reality is far more complicated than the models imply. Political factors are always present, and reality cannot be explained adequately without them. Then, too, such sharp distinctions between traded and nontraded goods are difficult to make in Caribbean economies where nontradeables themselves contain a large import content. These models are nevertheless useful because they provide a framework, however simplified, for analyzing the interaction of monetary, fiscal, and exchange-rate policies in dependent economies.

EXCHANGE-RATE POLICY

Pegged Exchange Rates

Although the assumption of infinite elasticity of supply is not applicable to the Caribbean, whose major exports are primary agricultural and mineral commodities, that part of the Mundell model which examines the effectiveness of monetary and fiscal policy under a fixed exchange rate is of particular relevance. Most Caribbean currencies are pegged to the U.S. dollar. Thus the exchange rate between Caribbean currencies and the U.S. dollar is fixed until such a time when Caribbean governments find it necessary to devalue or revalue their currencies.[12] Because the U.S. dollar has been floating since 1973, the exchange rate between Caribbean currencies and those of the rest of the world is governed by the exchange rates between the U.S. dollar and the rest-of-the-world currencies. In effect, the Caribbean operates within a world economy on a dual exchange-rate system—one directly fixed with the United States and the other indirectly flexible with the rest of the world.

Theoretically, a sustained decline of the U.S. dollar against European currencies would make Caribbean exports to Europe cheaper and Caribbean

imports from Europe more expensive. Assuming inflation rates in all countries
are about the same, this development would encourage the diversification of
Caribbean export markets toward Europe and the concentration of Caribbean
imports from the United States. The latter effect, of course, would be due to the
relatively lower cost of imports from the United States vis-a-vis Europe. This
would increase the Caribbean dependence on the United States for imports and
Caribbean demand for the U.S. dollar—a condition that could lead to
intermittent devaluations of weak currencies against the dollar.

The behavior of selected world currencies against the U.S. dollar for the
period 1965–78 is shown in Table 4.1. The German mark and the Japanese yen
have been steadily rising against the U.S. dollar, while the pound sterling has
been steadily declining. The Canadian dollar has shown modest fluctuations but
generally has remained stable. The long-run decline in the U.S. dollar price of
the pound sterling should therefore encourage Caribbean imports from
Britain—the second major trading partner of the larger Caribbean countries—
and discourage Caribbean exports to that country. On the other hand, the rising
dollar price for the German mark and the Japanese yen should have the opposite
effect. However, there are obviously a number of factors that may frustrate this

TABLE 4.1

Selected Foreign Exchange Rates, 1965–78 (in U.S. cents per unit of foreign currency)

Year	Germany	Canada	Japan	United Kingdom
1965	25.036	92.743	.27662	279.59
1966	25.007	92.811	.27598	279.30
1967	25.084	92.689	.27613	275.04
1968	25.048	92.801	.27735	239.35
1969	25.491	92.855	.27903	239.01
1970	27.424	95.802	.27921	239.59
1971	28.768	99.021	.28779	244.42
1972	31.364	100.937	.32995	250.08
1973	37.758	99.977	.36915	245.10
1974	38.723	102.257	.34302	234.03
1975	40.729	98.30	.33705	222.16
1976	39.737	101.41	.33741	180.48
1977	43.070	94.02	.37242	174.55
1978*	49.009	87.59	.45101	185.09

*April.
Source: Federal Reserve *Bulletin*; International Monetary Fund, *International Financial Statistics*.

TABLE 4.2

Caribbean Exchange Rates,[a] 1970–78
(in U.S. cents per unit of Caribbean currency)

Year	Jamaica	Trinidad and Tobago	Guyana	Barbados
1970	120.00	50.00	50.00	50.00
1971	121.73	50.63	50.48	50.76
1972	125.04	52.04	47.90	52.04
1973	110.00	51.04	47.01	51.04
1974	110.00	48.70	44.85	48.70
1975	110.00	46.08	42.45	49.50
1976	110.00	41.02	39.21	49.90
1977	110.00	41.66	39.21	49.83
1978[b]	95.24	41.66	39.21	49.96

[a]Par or Market Rates.
[b]April.
Source: International Monetary Fund, *International Financial Statistics*.

outcome, such as differential rates of inflation, transportation costs, tax policies, and a host of trade barriers.

Table 4.2 shows the behavior of Caribbean exchange rates for 1970–78. All currencies have declined in value against the U.S. dollar; as the U.S. dollar weakens against the major foreign currencies, Caribbean currencies pegged to the dollar become even weaker vis-a-vis such currencies as the German mark and Japanese yen.

This pegging of Caribbean currencies to the U.S. dollar results in a situation where the exchange-rate policy of the U.S. Federal Reserve system becomes by proxy the exchange-rate policy of the Caribbean vis-a-vis the rest of the world. While this arrangement may relieve the Caribbean central banks from having to engage in foreign exchange activity to support their currencies in the world market, it imposes upon them the need for appropriate domestic monetary and fiscal policies to stabilize domestic prices and to stimulate employment and growth. The extent to which the central banks manage their reserves effectively is critical to all these objectives. Courtney Blackman sums up the problem of reserve management for economic development as follows:

(1) The structural dependence of most LDCs [less-developed countries] on foreign trade means that balance of payments adjustments cannot prudently be left to marginal movements in the foreign exchange markets.

(2) Wild fluctuations in the export earnings of LDCs, together with a steady demand for imported necessities, require an inventory of foreign exchange reserves.

(3) Technological and financial dependence on the modern industrial economies requires continuous access to foreign exchange for current payments as well as for debt servicing.

(4) Once economic development is seen as a national priority, then foreign exchange earnings must be diverted from low priority uses and allocated to high priority items and to service foreign debts arising out of such transactions.[13]

Devaluation as an Adjustment Mechanism

A government committed to raising the level of welfare of the majority of its population that is poor strives vainly to insulate the domestic price of basic consumption and raw materials imports from the price-increasing effect of devaluation.* The harsh price adjustment required in a small open developing economy demands radical surgery to political programs designed to maximize vote-getting. Local politicians generally justify these adjustments by appearing to have them imposed on the government by an outside power such as the International Monetary Fund (IMF). The Jamaican situation is a classic example.

The stagnation of the Jamaican economy in the 1970s and the severe disequilbrium in the balance of payments which this created caused the Jamaican dollar to be devalued five times between 1973 and 1978. Over this period, the par rate of exchange with the U.S. dollar moved from (J) $1 = (U.S.) $1.20 to (J) $1 = (U.S.) $0.64. The devaluations in 1977 and 1978 were conditions imposed by the IMF for making soft loans available to help solve a desperate balance-of-payments situation. But the exchange rates to begin with were vastly overvalued and did not reflect the fundamental disequilibrium created by low productivity, lagging exports, slow growth rates, and high public consumption.

In January 1978, when the basic exchange rate of the Jamaican dollar was devalued by 15.5 percent, price increases in such basic food items as rice, flour, salt fish, and bread ranged from 85 percent to 21.4 percent. The 48 percent devaluation of the basic rate and the 15 percent devaluation of the special rate in May 1978 eliminated the dual exchange rate and established one rate of exchange with the U.S. dollar: (J) $1.55 = (U.S.) $1.00.

---

*As its balance-of-payments position deteriorated in 1977, Jamaica adopted a strategy of dual exchange rates: a basic (high) rate for the import of priority goods, and a special lower rate for the proceeds from exports.

This means that the price increases of basic items will be even larger. The January devaluation occurred when the IMF closed the window on its $70 million line of credit to Jamaica for failing to meet certain monetary policy conditions. The May devaluation was a condition for receiving a three-year loan of $240 million to shore up a dramatically deteriorated foreign exchange position. In addition to the devaluation, the IMF demanded a fiscal program that would eliminate the budget deficit and an incomes policy that would severely restrain wages. The fiscal requirement translated into an increase in taxes of over (J) $180 million for fiscal year 1978/79. The combined price effect of the devaluation and the new tax program created a phenomenal increase in prices. In a society where the great majority of the population is poor and where, since 1972, the socialist government has proliferated "people programs" designed to address the unequal distribution of income, the adjustment process will be particularly difficult because it will entail a redistribution of income in favor of the producers of internationally traded goods. An observation by Carl Stone regarding the conditions imposed by the IMF on Jamaica in January 1978 is critical of the IMF dealings with poor small countries:

> The IMF at this time is merely helping Third World countries to get foreign exchange to ensure that they would pay their debts to creditors of the rich capitalist countries. In the process they use the devaluation technique to force Third World countries to reduce their living standards by increasing the price of imports and cutting down on the use and consumption of imported goods. This may be good for the rich creditor countries, but hardly attempts to come to terms with the real problems of Third World economies. It pursues austerity with a view to improving the credit-worthiness of poor countries, but with no concern or interest in stimulating development or growth.[14]

The numerous economic packages introduced in Jamaica in the 1970s to facilitate the adjustment process have not worked. A primary feature of these packages is foreign exchange controls expressly administered to favor imports of essential food and materials and capital goods and to restrict the import of luxuries. Perhaps the best explanation of why this policy has not worked for Jamaica is provided by Harry Johnson:

> If a country seeks to make the composition of its imports conform to the pattern appropriate to a rapidly developing economy by rationing its scarce supply of foreign exchange so as to favor imports of essential food and materials and capital goods and inhibit imports of luxuries, it is likely to impede its economic development in two ways. Such a policy involves an implicit subsidy on imports of the essential goods, and tax on imports of the non-essential goods, by comparison with a situation of no controls on imports coupled with an equilibrium exchange rate. By relying on foreign exchange rationing instead of imposing an explicit tax on imports of non-essentials, the policy-makers miss the opportunity to appropriate the scarcity value of non-essential imports

created by rationing. Instead of adding to the tax revenue available for development, the scarcity rent is allocated to the recipients of import licenses (from whom it may be passed back as bribes to government employees), or, if domestic prices of imported goods are controlled to prevent abnormal profits, defused among the consumers of the goods in question. This is the first deleterious effect of exchange rationing on the rate of economic growth—the sacrifice of an opportunity to raise tax revenue. This sacrifice can be quite substantial, as is evidenced by the very high domestic prices (relative to foreign) of foreign-produced goods frequently observable in countries practising exchange control. If exchange control or import restriction were replaced by exchange auctioning or tariffs, the government could obtain the same effects on the pattern of imports while increasing the revenues available for financing development. This is the second major point that emerges from the experience of planned economic development; that fiscal policy methods are superior to direct control methods for shaping the balance of payments to conform to the requirements of an economic development policy.[15]

While chronic balance-of-payments problems forced Jamaica to devalue its currency, exchange-rate policy in Trinidad and Tobago moved in the opposite direction. In May 1976, Trinidad and Tobago unpegged its dollar from the pound sterling and pegged it to the U.S. dollar at a rate of (TT) $2.40 = (U.S.) $1.00. This represented a revaluation of the TT dollar from a market rate of (TT) $2.72 = (U.S.) $1.00. Two of the reasons given for the revaluation and the pegging to the U.S. dollar are: the changing patterns of trade and payments which primarily reflect a shift from sterling areas to the U.S. dollar areas; and the need to reduce the level of imported inflation and to remove uncertainties which were hampering the free flow of trade.[16]

DOMESTIC PRICES AND EXCHANGE-RATE CHANGES

The import price effect of exchange-rate changes is called the "pass through" effect. Mordecai Kreinin defines it as "the extent to which exchange rate changes are transferred into changes in prices of imports (denominated in the local currency) and exports (denominated in foreign currencies)."[17] The extent of the pass-through effect depends on the elasticity of the import demand by the devaluing country and the elasticity of the supply of exports facing that country. In general, "a small country, which can be assumed to face an infinitely (or very highly) elastic supply of exports from its trading partners is likely to experience a nearly complete pass-through on the import side."[18] (In the case of a large country like the United States, studies of the 1971–74 period have shown that approximately 15 to 30 percent of the price increases were attributed to the fall in the external value of the dollar.)[19]

If we view the pass-through effect of a devaluation as a tax, then the complete shifting of such a tax would be possible only if the demand for the imported consumption goods (or those produced with imported inputs) were perfectly inelastic. To the extent that imports contain a high share of necessities for consumption and for industrial and agricultural production, demand may be assumed to be highly inelastic and most of the "devaluation tax" may be expected to be shifted forward. Monetary policy, of course, must be sufficiently accommodating to allow such shifting to be effective. In other words, in order for the prices to rise by the amount of the devaluation, the money supply must grow. The government, however, may intervene to moderate the extent of shifting in the short run with fiscal action in the form of subsidies through price stabilization funds or state trading corporations. Such actions generally undermine the primary objective of devaluation, which is to improve the balance of payments.

INFLATION AND THE MONEY SUPPLY

In order to determine the extent to which domestic prices and money supply respond to changes in exogenously determined prices (import prices), a number of regressions were run using the log form

$$\text{Log } Y = a + b \text{ Log } X.$$

The elasticities of domestic prices (p^c) with respect to import prices (p^m), and the money supply (MS), and the elasticity of the money supply with respect to import prices are shown in Table 4.3.

All the elasticity coefficients are positive and significant. Equation 1 shows an elastic relationship between the money supply and import prices for all countries except Guyana. The elasticity coefficient in equation 2 was less than one for all countries; it was lowest for Guyana and highest for Barbados. This may very well reflect the differences in the degree of government control over economic activity in the two countries. The elasticity coefficient of equation 3 is also less than one for all countries; it is the most statistically significant of all, indicating the vulnerability of domestic prices to changes in import prices.

The foregoing also suggests that an increase in import prices increases the demand for money to spend on imports, requiring the monetary stock to adjust to meet this higher level of spending. As Robert Keleher argues, "in small, open economies, prices do not adjust to quantities of money but money adjusts via the balance of payments to the price level. Money in the small, open economy serves to accommodate inflation rather than to cause it."[20]

The subordination of monetary policy in Trinidad and Tobago to fiscal policy and balance of payments can be illustrated for the period 1974–76. Despite the tightening up of hire-purchase (installment–plan) credit beginning in 1973, and the increase in the statutory reserve requirement to 9 percent in 1974 in an attempt to control inflationary pressures, money supply expanded at an accelerated rate during 1976. The explanation provided by the Ministry of Finance is that "the money supply is determined by the movements in net foreign

TABLE 4.3

Regression Results of the Relationship between the Consumer Price Index, the Import Price Index, and the Index of Money Supply

Equation		A	Log MS	Log P^m	R^2
		Jamaica (1965–75)			
1	Log MS	− .628		+ 1.18	.87
				(7.92)	
2	Log P^c	.772	+ .593		.93
			(11.76)		
3	Log P^c	.470		+ .76	.97
				(20.15)	
		Trinidad and Tobago (1967–74)			
1	Log MS	− .517		+ 1.25	.74
				(4.12)	
2	Log P^c	1.22	.416		.92
			(8.53)		
3	Log P^c	.86		+ .589	.88
				(8.0)	
		Barbados (1965–74)			
1	Log MS	− .521		+ 1.14	.78
				(5.33)	
2	Log P^c	.292	.816		.73
			(4.71)		
3	Log P^c	.653		.717	.95
				(13.06)	
		Guyana (1965–74)			
1	Log MS	.249		.945	.79
				(5.55)	
2	Log P^c	2.791	.385		.90
			(9.29)		
3	Log P^c	2.786		.402	.97
				(18.34)	

Source: Computations are based on data in Tables D.14, D.15, and D.16.

assets and net domestic assets. Since 1974 both variables have responded to the stimulus of increased Government deposits with the banking system, which have risen principally as a result of the growth of Government revenue from oil taxation."[21] Thus the impact of higher prices for exports and the government's fiscal action on the money supply more than offset the tightening of credit as a counterinflationary measure. The net effect was an adjustment of the money stock to sustain the high rate of inflation.

Under a regime of fixed exchange rates, it is impossible for domestic price levels to remain constant for a foreign-trade-dependent price-taker when foreign prices are rising. When domestic prices are rigid downward,* any attempt to use tight monetary policy to choke off price increases and to maintain equilibrium in the balance of payments will create unemployment. Political imperative in the Caribbean requires the use of expansionary fiscal policy to increase employment and consumption. To accommodate this, the money supply automatically expands to meet the increased government and private demand for money. This in turn increases the import bill, intensifies domestic inflation, and worsens the balance of payments by reducing foreign exchange reserves. Thus the transmission of higher import prices into high domestic prices is facilitated by an expansion of the money stock.† This path is clearly self-defeating because ultimately a deteriorating balance of payments will dictate a devaluation of the currency which will further increase the price of imports. The vicious cycle will continue and public internal and external indebtedness will grow by leaps and bounds. At this stage, draconian measures are required to break the spiral.

FISCAL POLICY

At the heart of the transition from colonialism to independence is the evolution of budget policy as the major instrument of development. Under British colonialism, public finance was constrained by a laissez-faire philosophy that was devoid of any strategy for development. With a low taxable capacity and a high dependence on colonial loans and grants from the mother country, restraint on the growth of government was achieved through a balanced budget. The existing financial institutional setting made deficit financing a rarity before the end of World War II. The absence of a central bank provided no domestic money-creating capability and local colonial governments had no more ability to borrow than a business firm.

---

*A number of factors contribute to the downward rigidity of prices: monopolistic structure of local production; the power of labor unions; the multiplicity of links in the local distribution chain; and general inefficiency.

†The expansion of the money supply is frequently induced by government borrowing from the central bank.

Independence brought with it the need for a strategy of development and a larger role for public finance. The development goals grew with the changing demographics and ideology of the region and outpaced the growth of taxable capacity. New monetary institutions were created to facilitate the mobilization of resources for development in general and to support the ends of public finance in particular.

Within 15 years of independence, the burden of growth and development has fallen disproportionately on public finance and the role of government has grown phenomenonally in the Caribbean (see Table 4.4). The larger role of government in the Caribbean economies also includes the function of economic stabilization. Fiscal policy for stabilization is generally of greater importance in the developed countries, especially in the United States, despite the fact that in the small open Caribbean economies, economic instability is a common characteristic of their foreign trade dependence.

Unlike the situation in developed countries, the ability of fiscal policy in developing countries in general and in the Caribbean in particular to execute effective stabilization policies is constrained by the income inelasticity of the tax structure. This is because average incomes are low and progressive income taxes account for a smaller share of total tax revenues than in, say, the United States. Tax structures in the Caribbean therefore provide limited automatic stabili-

TABLE 4.4

Public Expenditure as a Percent of Gross Domestic Product, 1973-76.

Year	Jamaica (J $ million)			Trinidad (TT $ million)		
	Total Government Expenditures[a]	Gross Domestic Product[b]	Expenditures as Percent of GDP	Total Government Expenditures[a]	Gross Domestic Product[c]	Expenditures as Percent of GDP
1973	362.9	1,709.1	21.2	573.5	2,467.5	23.2
1974	471.1	2,244.6	21.0	1,301.3	3,799.0	34.3
1975	728.0	2,653.3	27.4	1,681.5	4,959.3	33.9
1976	974.2	2,768.0	35.2	2,024.1	5,607.0	35.7

[a]Includes recurrent and capital expenditures.
[b]Purchasers' values at current prices.
[c]Factor cost at current prices.
Sources: *Economic and Social Survey Jamaica 1973, 1975* (Kingston: The Government Printer, 1974, 1976); Trinidad, *Accounting for the Petrodollar* (Port-of-Spain: Central Statistical Office, 1977); *Gross Domestic Product of the Republic of Trinidad and Tobago 1966-1976* (Port-of-Spain: Central Statistics Office, 1977); International Monetary Fund, *International Financial Statistics.*

zation. Further, such automatic stabilizers as unemployment insurance and retirement payments are only in their rudimentary stages of development. Thus economic stabilization is left to discretionary fiscal policy supported by monetary, exchange rate, and prices and incomes policies.

Because of the high degree of foreign trade dependence of Caribbean countries, fiscal policy for stabilization is essentially a reaction to changes in the international economy. And it has generally tended to be employment-oriented in good times and in bad because of the persistent poverty and high unemployment rates in these countries.

The experience of Barbados during the 1974 recession in the United States and other Western capitalist countries is a useful example. In his budget speech to Parliament in November 1974, Prime Minister Barrow said: "It must be frankly recognized that the prospects for an early resumption of growth in Barbados depend to a large extent on the success or failure of the international economic community, in particular the major economic powers, in overcoming the very severe problems we all face."[22]

In spite of this expression of helplessness, the prime minister viewed the relationship between Barbados and the major economic powers as one of interdependence—a relationship which "requires that we should do our part in introducing corrective and remedial action."[23] Corrective and remedial action here means primarily the use of fiscal policy to restrain inflation and to bolster sagging production. But in Barbados, fiscal policy by itself is virtually helpless to restrain inflation—which is largely imported—and to stimulate production—which is largely export-oriented.

The result of the Barbados government's fiscal exercise was a substantial increase in the budget deficit resulting from increases in current expenditures. This in turn produced a fiscal position which was "at once inflationary (price) and deflationary (output and employment)"[24] and prompted the prime minister to call for a magical "package of policies designed to reduce the current high level of inflation while at the same time raising the level of investment as a necessary precondition to the resumption of economic growth."[25]

In its fight against the recession, which was principally induced by rapid increases in oil prices engineered by the Organization of Petroleum Exporting Countries (OPEC), and its struggle to finance ambitious public programs, Jamaica used its leverage as the major supplier of bauxite to the United States to increase its bauxite revenues substantially. Although this was not purely a countercyclical measure, it had the effect of temporarily improving the local fiscal situation and postponing the inevitable balance-of-payments crisis fed by a stagnant economy and an overvalued currency.

The fiscal options in the Caribbean are limited because the growth of local tax bases is inextricably tied to the performance of the narrowly based and foreign-dominated export sector. And the taking over of export industries does not assure an expansion of taxable capacity. If anything, taxable capacity for Jamaica and Guyana has shrunk in the 1970s.

PRICE CONTROLS

Since the burden of inflation is inevitably borne by the great masses of poor people in developing countries, price controls have become an integral feature of Caribbean political economy. This situation is expressed succinctly by the governor of the Barbados Central Bank in his address to the first graduating class of price inspectors: "The purpose of price control in Barbados should be to ensure that the poorer classes in the society are not called upon to shoulder more than their just burden in our national drive for economic development."[26] Because the unrestricted operation of the market may establish equilibrium prices which are socially and politically unacceptable to Caribbean governments, there has been an accelerated growth in their reliance on price controls in recent years. And since price controls are usually accompanied by a panoply of other controls, the growth of government bureaucracy has been phenomenal. This rapid growth in the size of the bureaucracy has led Blackman to caution that "developing countries must be extremely careful that bureaucratic controls do not consume scarce administrative resources which might be better used for other purposes."[27]

In Jamaica, the role of the Prices Commission has grown by leaps and bounds. A sample of the commission's activities in 1975 is illustrative of that growth:

> . . . over 26,000 routine visits were made to business establishments and in excess of 4,600 test purchases made by price inspectors. The number of complaints investigated totalled 334. These activities resulted in 1,065 prosecutions for breaches of the Trade Law. The Research and Analytical Division of the Commission completed 122 reports on applications for price increases.[28]

The expansion of the commission's role that year required an additional staff of 67 persons.

In Trinidad, where the inflation rate has been the lowest of the four Caribbean countries, there was no less urgency about the control of prices. The Prices Commission was strengthened by the Permanent Advisory Council, which was created at the National Consultation on Prices held in July 1972. "This body maintains its own surveillance on prices in the country and expresses an independent opinion on acceptability of proposed price changes; its views are given full weight not only by the Prices Commission but also by the Cabinet."[29] The government was also studying "the feasibility of fixing, in advance, ceiling prices and price increases for certain basic consumer goods."[30]

CRUEL DILEMMAS

Employment versus Inflation

The small open developing Caribbean economy, as we have seen, is in a no-win situation. Recession cum inflation in metropolitan countries presents such an economy with almost impossible stabilization problems. Ideally, it should engage in counterrecessionary fiscal policy to generate development, and, at the same time, it should try to achieve equilibrium in the balance of payments through a tight money policy. But this leads to the classic Meade-Mundell "dilemma" case where monetary policy aimed at maintaining balance-of-payments equilibrium generates unemployment, and fiscal policy aimed at maintaining high employment generates a balance-of-payments deficit.[31]

As foreign exchange reserves deteriorate, pressure builds up for a devaluation of the currency. Devaluation in turn increases domestic prices. Theoretically, the adjustment process would require imports to decline and exports to rise, since exports would become relatively cheaper. If import demand is inelastic, the demand for money will increase to maintain imports and the money stock will adjust accordingly. The net effect is domestic inflation. Monetary policy must expand to accommodate inflation and fiscal policy must expand to create employment.

It is this cruel dilemma which makes price and exchange controls such an integral part of modern-day Caribbean economic policy. The achievement of internal economic stability and development in this context requires what Heller calls "an uncommon fusion of political will and economic skill; (a) will, for example, to resist a high propensity to import consumer goods, especially luxuries; and (b) skill not only in managing tax and exchange rates but also in so timing the changes and channeling the proceeds as to promote stable and balanced economic development."[32]

Exports versus Import Substitution

The subservience of domestic economic policies to external developments is implied in the argument that developed countries should pursue expansionary policies that will increase the demand for the exports of developing countries. An editorial in the North American edition of Jamaica's leading newspaper, The *Gleaner*, for example, sees the slow economic growth and restrictive import policies of the advanced countries as a major cause of Jamaica's balance-of-payments difficulties.

> If the main industrialized countries could stimulate their economies sufficiently this would help to provide the needed impetus. However the reappearance of increasing rates of inflation in the United States, and its

depressing effect on investment, the prospects for improvement in demand, at least in the short-run, for Jamaica's main exports are dim.[33]

This general proposition is supported by Irma Adelman when she argues that

on balance, it would appear that a higher rate of growth of U.S. GDP would contribute to the growth of LDCs by providing export markets and a world economic climate more conducive to internal development and economic restructuring. In the process, it would, at least in the short-to-intermediate term, make more adverse, on the average, the balance of payments of the non-OPEC LDCs. This latter effect, however, is not likely to inhibit LDC growth so long as the developed world is in a state of economic expansion.[34]

One of the dangers of the slowdown of economic growth in the United States, Adelman argues, is that the developing countries

generally would be forced to adopt, as rapidly as possible, an import-substitution policy.

Unfortunately, import substitution, except in foodstuffs, hurts both growth and distribution. The deterioration in distribution is due to the fact that nonfood import substitution reduces the relative price of rural versus urban goods, thus lowering the incomes (both relatively and absolutely) of the rural poor. Since the rural poor are, in general, poorer than the urban poor, the resultant change in the rural-urban terms of trade would degrade the overall distribution of income and would increase the overall extent of poverty. The worsening of the agricultural terms of trade for the farmers is due to several processes. First of all, nonfood import substitution makes urban manufacturers more expensive. Second, by raising manufacturing costs, it leads to reduce output, lowering the rate of growth of urban incomes and decreasing the relative rate of urban demand for food. Third, the reduced manufacturing output decreases the rate of absorption of would-be rural immigrants into urban employment, thus contributing to continued pressures on land and to unchanged agricultural output in the face of a lower urban demand growth rate. The end result of these processes is a drastic deterioration in the agricultural terms of trade and therefore in income distribution.

If U.S. policy is to encourage economic growth with equity in the LDCs, in preference simply to overall LDC economic growth, it is clear that the U.S. should not participate in economic policies that are likely to force the LDCs to import substitution.[35]

Thus the pursuit of high-growth-rate strategies by the United States and the Organisation for Economic Co-operation and Development (OECD) countries would generally have a favorable impact not only on the growth of income in poor countries but on the distribution of income as well.

Adelman has come down in favor of a strategy of growth based on labor-intensive exports as opposed to a strategy of import substitution. The latter, she argues, will adversely affect growth and income distribution and therefore increase poverty, while the former will create more employment and reduce poverty. But the prisoner's dilemma for countries like the Caribbean is that

> it is presently the labor-intensive export-oriented development strategy, unfortunately, that would be virtually precluded in the climate of (relatively) shrinking world incomes, trade, and aid that would result from less rapid growth rate in the industrial countries and the consequent slower growth of demand for inputs.[36]

A policy that would stimulate high growth rates in the United States coupled with a strategy of labor-intensive export growth in the Caribbean may even reduce the propensity of Caribbean workers to migrate to the United States. But the development of labor-intensive exports in the Caribbean, and particularly in Jamaica, is faced with some formidable institutional constraints such as minimum wage laws, aggressive labor unions, and a national insurance tax which is in part a tax on the employment of labor. Even if the appropriate technology and capital were available, the institutional setting would present serious problems.

NOTES

1. Bent Hansen, *The Economic Theory of Fiscal Policy* (London: George Allen & Unwin, 1967), pp. 388–429.
2. Ibid., p. 398.
3. Ibid., p. 399.
4. Ibid., p. 397.
5. Not only is there a de facto subservience of monetary policy to fiscal policy but a de jure subservience as well. This is illustrated in Section 39 of the Bank of Jamaica Law, 1960, which states that

> the Minister [of Finance] may from time to time after consultation with the Governor [of the Central Bank] give the Bank in writing such directions of a general nature as appear to the Minister to be necessary in the public interest, including without prejudice the state of credit in any sector of the economy and either to make recommendations for improving the supply of credit or to take steps to foster the provision of credit to that sector of the economy.

In the deliberations of the House of Representatives leading to the establishment of the Bank of Jamaica, the minister of finance underscored the subservience of the central bank to the Government:

> . . . we are determined that the Central Bank is not going to be allowed to achieve any independent position of power qua the Government of the country, and that is why it will

be left to carry out its several duties under the Government and the Board. And when it comes to matters of overall credit policy, the Bank must then realise it must take its direction in those general matters from the Government of the country.

Quoted in Charles V. Callender, *The Development of the Capital Market Institutions in Jamaica* (Kingston: Institute for Social and Economic Research, University of the West Indies, 1965) from Jamaica *Hansard,* Proceedings of the House of Representatives 1960–61, p. 309.

6. R. A. Mundell, "Capital Mobility and Stabilization Policy Under Fixed and Flexible Exchange Rates," *Canadian Journal of Economics and Political Science* 29 (1963): 475–85.

7. Martin F. J. Prachowny, *Small Open Economies* (Lexington, Mass.: D. C. Heath, 1975), p. 88.

8. M. June Flanders and Elahanan Helpman, "On Exchange Rate Policies for a Small Country," *Economic Journal* 88 (1978): 44–58.

9. Ibid., pp. 51–52.

10. Ibid., p. 55.

11. Ibid.

12. The particular rate at which a currency is pegged to another will depend upon a number of factors. As Blackman puts it, "in fixing an exchange rate, the decision-maker must weigh the effects of different exchange rate levels on export earnings, on the cost of imports, on the domestic price level, on the foreign debt and on income distribution." Courtney N. Blackman, "Managing Reserves for Development," *Columbia Journal of World Business* 11 (1976): 38.

13. Ibid., p. 37.

14. Carl Stone, "IMF Pressure Brought to Bear," *Jamaica Weekly Gleaner (NA)*, January 18, 1978, p. 8.

15. Harry G. Johnson, "Fiscal Policy and the Balance of Payments," in *Government Finance and Economic Development*, ed. Alan T. Peacock and Gerald Hauser (Paris: Organisation for Economic Co-operation and Development, 1965), pp. 163–64.

16. Trinidad and Tobago, *Review of the Economy 1976 Trinidad and Tobago* (Port-of-Spain: C.S.O. Printing Unit, 1976).

17. Mordecai E. Kreinin, "The Effect of Exchange Rates Changes on the Prices and Volume of Foreign Trade," *IMF Staff Papers* 24 (1977): 297.

18. Ibid., p. 298.

19. Joint Economic Committee, Congress of the United States, *Achieving Price Stability Through Economic Growth* (Washington, D.C.: Government Printing Office, 1974), pp. 27–28.

20. Robert E. Keleher, "A Framework for Examining the Small, Open Regional Economy: An Application of the Macroeconomics of Open Systems," paper presented at the Western Economic Association Meetings, Honolulu, June 24, 1978.

21. Trinidad and Tobago, op. cit., p. 54.

22. Errol W. Barrow, *Supplementary Financial Statement and Budget Proposals* (Bridgetown: Government Printing Office, 1974), p. 2.

23. Ibid.

24. Ibid., p. 10.

25. Ibid.

26. Courtney N. Blackman, "Price Control within the Context of a Developing Economy," *Central Bank of Barbados Quarterly Report* 3 (1976): 29.

27. Blackman, "Managing Reserves for Development," op. cit., p. 39.

28. Jamaica, *Economic and Social Survey Jamaica 1975* (Kingston: National Planning Agency, 1976), p. 61.

29. G. M. Chambers, *Budget Speech 1973* (Port-of-Spain: Government Printery, 1973), pp. 22–23.

30. Ibid., p. 23.

31. Flanders and Helpman, op. cit., p. 148.

32. Walter W. Heller, "Fiscal Policies for Underdeveloped Countries," in *Readings on Taxation in Developing Countries* ed. Richard M. Bird and Oliver Oldman (Baltimore: Johns Hopkins University Press, 1975), p. 17.

33. *Jamaica Weekly Gleaner (NA)*, May 8, 1978, p. 13.

34. Irma Adelman, "Interaction of U.S. and Foreign Economic Growth Rates and Patterns," in *U.S. Economic Growth from 1976–1986: Prospects, Problems, and Patterns—Economic Growth in the International Context*, Vol. 12, Joint Economic Committee, Congress of the United States (Washington, D.C.: Government Printing Office, 1977), p. 5.

35. Ibid., p. 6.

36. Ibid., p. 7.

5

Dependence and Foreign Capital Flows

CAPITAL FLOWS AND THE PUBLIC DEBT

For small open developing economies, the balance of payments is the critical barometer of their domestic condition. The ability of exports to finance the import of consumption and capital goods determines the magnitude of the balance-of-payments deficit or surplus. The condition of the balance of payments in turn influences exchange-rate policy as well as domestic fiscal and monetary policy.

For the Caribbean, with the exception of Trinidad, which has gained immense benefit from the sharp increase in the price of oil in 1973, the scenario has been one of rising balance-of-payments deficits financed by a drastic reduction in foreign exchange reserves and by foreign borrowing. Table 5.1 shows the deficit on current account for the four Caribbean countries in the period 1970–76. In 1974, substantially increased tax revenues from bauxite exports and the rising export price of sugar dramatically reduced the deficit for Jamaica and Guyana, while the increase in oil prices provided Trinidad with a large surplus. (This same oil increase and its resultant worldwide recession cum inflation triggered marked deterioration of the balance-of-payments position of other Caribbean countries.)

The composition of the long-term capital inflow to finance this deficit is probably the best indicator of the changing political and economic strategies in the Caribbean. Between 1970 and 1976, long-term capital inflow into Jamaica and Guyana became almost exclusively debt capital, that is, government borrowing (see Table 5.1). This completely reversed the situation that existed up until 1970. The complete disappearance of foreign private direct investment flows to Jamaica and Guyana in the 1970s may be attributed to the diminished

TABLE 5.1

Balance of Payments, 1970–76
($ million)

	Current Account[a]			
Year	Jamaica	Guyana	Trinidad and Tobago	Barbados
1970	− 152.9	− 21.1	− 79.8	− 41.7
1971	− 172.2	− 5.8	− 137.7	− 35.3
1972	− 196.7	− 15.4	− 161.4	− 42.9
1973	− 247.6	− 63.4	− 26.3	− 52.0
1974	− 91.9	− 9.1	271.0	− 48.1
1975	− 282.8	− 23.4	277.7	− 41.5
1976	− 302.7	− 139.6	144.0	− 56.9

	Capital Account				
Year	Long-term Capital (nie)[b]	Direct Investment	Other Government	Other	Short-term Capital (nie)[b]
			Jamaica		
1970	160.7	161.4	− 4.4	3.7	− 0.4
1971	188.4	176.0	3.1	9.2	− 13.3
1972	126.7	97.8	15.4	13.5	44.1
1973	206.2	75.1	33.1	98.0	7.2
1974	225.6	23.3	85.4	116.9	− 48.8
1975	204.9	− 1.8	121.8	85.0	70.7
1976	87.7	− 0.6	77.4	11.0	− 37.2
			Guyana		
1970	15.8	9.0	7.0	− 0.2	− 0.2
1971	15.3	− 55.8	63.8	7.3	− 3.2
1972	15.3	2.5	7.3	5.5	0.1
1973	32.1	8.2	13.7	10.1	− 4.1
1974	43.4	1.3	15.9	26.2	4.8
1975	69.1	0.8	20.9	47.4	− 3.9
1976	36.7	− 0.6	10.2	27.1	5.8

(Continued)

TABLE 5.1 *(Continued)*

	Capital Account				
Year	Long-term Capital (nie)[b]	Direct Investment	Other Government	Other	Short-term Capital (nie)[b]
		Trinidad and Tobago			
1970	83.3	83.2	− 2.2	2.3	− 4.3
1971	126.6	103.3	15.5	7.7	− 5.0
1972	105.2	86.6	21.2	− 2.6	9.3
1973	65.0	65.6	35.0	− 35.6	10.7
1974	65.5	84.7	− 31.1	12.0	− 45.6
1975	229.7	231.3	− 1.6	−	− 18.7
1976	159.4	248.7	− 24.2	− 65.0	− 15.9
		Barbados			
1970	12.2	8.4	0.3	3.5	0.8
1971	16.7	15.0	0.0	1.7	2.0
1972	21.0	18.7	2.6	− 0.3	− 1.8
1973	20.7	4.8	17.9	− 1.9	8.1
1974	3.8	2.3	1.1	0.5	1.1
1975	25.1	22.2	− 0.4	3.3	3.5
1976	22.1	6.1	2.7	13.3	4.6

[a]Goods and services and transfers.
[b]not included elsewhere.
Source: International Monetary Fund, *International Financial Statistics*, October 1977.

role of private enterprise in the development strategies of the two governments. Prime Minister Manley served notice that in his development strategy for Jamaica, foreign capital will become more "public and institutional." This became a self-fulfilling prophecy, for the disappearance of private capital flows forced the government to rely on public and institutional sources of foreign capital.

Caribbean governments must now create the jobs which would have been created by private direct foreign capital; and they must now substitute government consumption for private consumption foregone. To do this, the growth of government expenditures had to be accelerated to the point where it far outstripped the growth of tax revenues. The result has been an unprecedented increase in government budget deficits. The combination of budget deficits with the persistent balance-of-trade deficit has sharply increased the public debt in the 1970s. This has become a great burden on the economy because the large debt-service payments have imposed a substantial claim on scarce tax resources.

This is illustrated in Table 5.2, which compares debt charges as a percent of tax revenues for the United States, Jamaica, Guyana, and Barbados. (The United States is included merely to point up the higher debt burden of the Caribbean countries.) The debt burden is highest in Guyana, where it exceeded 31 percent in 1973; despite its decline in 1974 and 1975, it was almost 28 percent in 1976.

If all the debt were internal, we could argue that all the interest payments are made to nationals and that this represents a source of national income and tax revenues. Unlike the U.S. national debt, however, a substantial share of Caribbean debt is external, so that the debt burden is not only a claim against tax revenues but a claim against international reserves as well. Between 1970 and 1976, the external component of the total debt averaged 38.4 percent for Jamaica and 58.6 percent for Guyana. Table 5.3 shows the foreign debt charges as percentages of exports and international reserves. For the 1970–76 period, an average of 2.7 percent of the foreign exchange earned from Jamaica's exports was claimed by debt charges on the foreign debt.

Table 5.4 shows that the growth of the Jamaican external debt sharply increased the share of external debt charges in the total investment income outflow. From a little over 14 percent in 1971–72, this share rose to over 45 percent in 1975.

TABLE 5.2

Public Debt Charges as a Percent of Current Revenues, 1970–76

Year	United States	Jamaica*	Guyana	Barbados
1970	9.4	11.8	12.9	5.4
1971	10.4	9.3	14.5	3.6
1972	9.8	11.8	16.7	4.5
1973	9.8	11.6	31.1	8.6
1974	10.6	15.6	18.6	9.7
1975	11.0	13.9	15.0	8.7
1976	11.6	12.3	27.7	9.8

*Fiscal year, April 1 to March 31.

Sources: *Economic Report of the President*, January 1978; Bank of Guyana, *Economic Bulletin*, No. 10, October 1976; *Economic and Social Survey Jamaica 1970 to 1975* (Kingston: The Government Printer, 1971 to 1976); *Annual Statistical Digest* (Bridgetown: Central Bank of Barbados, 1975).

TABLE 5.3

Interest Payments on the External Debt as a Percentage of Exports and International Reserves, Jamaica, 1970–76

Year	Interest on External Debt (J $ million)	Interest as a Percent of Exports of Goods and Services	Interest as a Percent of Net International Reserves
1970	11.8	2.7	12.3
1971	12.3	2.6	9.3
1972	14.3	2.6	15.3
1973	16.3	2.8	21.4
1974	23.6	2.6	18.1
1975	30.9	3.0	27.0
1976	32.5	3.8	110.3

Sources: *Economic and Social Survey Jamaica 1973; 1975; 1976* (Kingston: The Government Printer, 1974; 1976; 1977); International Monetary Fund, *International Financial Statistics*, October 1977.

THE RECYCLING OF FINANCIAL CAPITAL

For Jamaica, during the period 1971–75, the outflow of investment income represented an average of 50 percent of capital inflow (Table 5.5); in 1972, this percentage reached as high as 85.8 percent. However, when we look at external debt charges in relation to official capital inflows (government borrowing), the percentage of these charges declined markedly between 1971–75, due to the sharp increase in government borrowing. What all this indicates is that there has been a two-way flow of capital: an outward flow in the form of investment income and an inward flow of debt and equity capital—mostly debt since 1972. The point remains, however, that a substantial share of new foreign capital inflow is financed by the income generated by old capital. Thus the inflow of foreign debt and equity capital sets in motion a perpetual recycling process where the developing country finds itself in the odd position of supplying a large part of the foreign capital it receives.

Over the period 1966 to 1976, net private direct investment flows to Jamaica from the United States totalled $423 million. As Table 5.6 indicates, this flow declined sharply after 1971. In 1976 it was a negative $83 million, largely reflecting the liquidation of some operations and the sale of ownership interests in the bauxite and hotel industries to the Jamaican government. The amount of profits repatriated to the United States over the 1966–76 period totalled $856 million, or 96 percent of total adjusted earnings. The total amount of profits repatriated was twice the amount of net direct investment flows. Only 4 percent of adjusted earnings were reinvested in Jamaica, compared to 31.5 percent for developing countries and 53 percent for developed countries (see Table 5.7). This supports the contention that the local economy has not benefited as much as it could have from the investment of U.S. multinational corporations. The most alarming fact is that investment income outflow to the United States was twice the size of direct investment flows from the United States to Jamaica. Thus Jamaica—which is a capital-poor developing country—finds itself a net exporter of private capital to the United States, where capital is relatively abundant.

This anomaly is also evident in Trinidad and Tobago, as well as in Guyana (see Tables 5.8 and 5.9). For the years 1971–76, U.S. net direct investment flows to Trinidad and Tobago totalled $436 million, while the outflow of investment income to U.S. investors totalled $524 million, making that country a net

TABLE 5.4

Public Debt, Jamaica and Guyana, 1970–76[a]

Year	Internal	External	Total	External Debt as a Percent of Total
		Jamaica (J $ million)		
1970	172.1	102.9	275.0	37.4
1971	210.3	110.0	320.3	34.3
1972	256.8	127.6	384.4	33.2
1973	308.4	159.6	468.0	34.1
1974	342.5	272.4	614.9	44.3
1975	456.7	385.3	842.0	45.8
1976	610.2[b]	399.6[b]	1,009.8	39.6
		Guyana (G $ million)		
1970	234.4	158.2	392.6	40.3
1971	275.9	163.7	439.6	37.2
1972	333.9	199.2	533.1	37.4
1973	370.2	255.7	625.9	40.8
1974	387.3	241.4	628.7	38.4
1975	411.7	215.7	627.4	34.4
1976	462.2	155.3	617.5	25.1

[a]Figures are provisional and represent the gross debt as of May 1976.
[b]Bank of Jamaica, *Statistical Digest*, October 1976.
Source: International Monetary Fund, *International Financial Statistics*, October 1977.

TABLE 5.5

Relationship between Investment Income Outflow and Long-Term Capital Inflow in Jamaica, 1971–75
(J $ million)

	Capital Investment Inflow			Net Investment Income Outflow		
Year	Official	Private	Total	External Debt Charges	Other	Total
1971	4.0	156.2	160.2	12.3	73.4	85.7
1972	18.6	98.4	117.0	14.3	86.1	100.4
1973	107.4	17.3	124.7	16.3	36.5	52.8
1974	150.1	71.0	221.1	21.0	40.5	61.5
1975	160.0	8.0	168.0	20.0	64.3	84.3

Source: *Economic and Social Survey Jamaica 1973 to 1975* (Kingston: The Government Printer, 1974 to 1976).

exporter of private capital to the United States. Only 6 percent of adjusted earnings were reinvested in Trinidad and Tobago for that period.

The picture for Guyana is more extreme, although the magnitude of the figures is smaller. The period 1969–76 was one of general disinvestment by U.S. private firms in the country. Since it became a Cooperative Republic in 1970, Guyana has vigorously pursued a policy of nationalization of the major foreign-dominated industries, including bauxite—which accounted for its major share of U.S. direct investment. Net private direct investment flows from the United States to Guyana for the seven-year period were a negative $19 million, and total investment income outflow to the United States was $11 million. This means that a total of $30 million flowed from Guyana to the United States during the period. There will undoubtedly be continued outflow of investment income from the remaining U.S. direct investment, and Guyana will for sometime remain a net exporter of capital to the United States, even though the magnitude may be quite small.

Barbados appears to be an exception to the general rule (see Table 5.10). For the period 1971–76, its total private direct investment flow from the United States exceeded the amount of profits repatriated to the United States by $5 million. Thus Barbados was a net importer of private capital from the United States. As we indicated in Chapter 3, U.S. private direct investment in Barbados is minuscule compared to that in Jamaica and Trinidad and Tobago. Since 1972

Investment Income Outflow as a Percent of Capital Inflow	External Debt Charges as a Percent of Official Capital Inflow	External Debt Charges as a Percent of Investment Income Outflow
53.5	307.5	14.4
85.8	76.9	14.2
42.3	15.2	30.8
27.8	14.0	34.0
50.1	12.5	45.6

the amount has leveled off at around $20 million. This means that the repatriation of profits to the United States in the years ahead will quite likely exceed the net private capital flows from the United States.

The small share of reinvested earnings in these developing economies perpetuates the need for new capital inflows to do what a larger share of reinvested earnings could accomplish. But a larger share of reinvested earnings would eventually reduce the dependence of the Caribbean on new investment capital inflow by breaking the recycling pattern. Some economists argue that the small share of earnings reinvested is part of an imperialist design to perpetuate the dependence of the Caribbean on the United States. [1] The current strategies of the localization of ownership and control of foreign-dominated industries are regarded by Caribbean governments as a major step toward accomplishing this goal.

If only a small portion of the profits from direct investment is reinvested, then an even smaller portion of the income from portfolio investment is likely to be reinvested. Thus the countries that are forced to rely on foreign debt capital may find it more difficult to break the recycling pattern in the absence of a moratorium on debt-service payments.

While Trinidad and Tobago is pursuing its strategy of localization of ownership and control within a capitalist context, Jamaica and Guyana are doing it in a socialist context. The result is that Trinidad and Tobago is able to continue to attract large inflows of U.S. private capital, while Jamaica and Guyana are dependent upon debt capital from the United States. The Trinidad

TABLE 5.6

U.S. Direct Investment, Net Flows of Capital and Income, Jamaica, 1966–76 ($ million)

Year	Net Capital Flows (1)	Reinvested Earnings (2)	Receipts of Income (3)	Adjusted Earnings (4)	Direct Investment (5)	Rate of Return (4) ÷ (5) (6)	(2) as Percent of (4)
1966	39	2	73	75	163	46.0	2.6
1967	40	2	77	79	204	38.7	2.5
1968	90	2	70	72	295	24.4	2.7
1969	92	4	87	91	392	23.2	4.4
1970	114	2	84[a]	86[b]	507	16.9	2.3
1971	107	4	77	81	618	13.1	4.9
1972	6	0	71	71	624	11.3	0.0
1973	− 9	4	79	83	618	13.4	4.8
1974	− 12	6	92	98	609	16.0	6.1
1975	− 39	7	79	86	654	13.1	8.1
1976	− 83	4	67	71	577	12.3	5.6
Total	423	37	856	893			

[a]This figure was not provided in the original data. It is imputed from the difference between Adjusted Earnings and Reinvested Savings.
[b]This figure was not provided in the original data. It was estimated as the arithmetic mean of the total Adjusted Earnings for 1969 and 1971.
Source: U.S. Department of Commerce, Bureau of Economic Analysis.

TABLE 5.7

Selected Data on U.S. Direct Investment in Jamaica and in Developed and Developing Countries, 1975 and 1976 ($ million)

Item	1975	1976
Jamaica		
1 Net capital flows	39	− 83
2 Reinvested earnings	7	4
3 Receipts of income	79	67
4 Adjusted earnings	86	70
5 Direct investment	654	577
6 Percent of rate of return	13.1	12.1
7 Reinvested earnings as a percent of adjusted earnings	8.8	5.7
Developed Countries		
1 Net capital flows	2,898	3,354
2 Reinvested earnings	4,900	6,176
3 Receipts of income	4,609	5,217
4 Adjusted earnings	9,509	11,393
5 Direct investment	90,923	101,159
6 Percent of rate of return	10.9	11.9
7 Reinvested earnings as a percent of adjusted earnings	51.5	54.2
Developing Countries		
1 Net capital flows	3,702	1,665
2 Reinvested earnings	3,083	1,204
3 Receipts of income	3,619	5,763
4 Adjusted earnings	6,703	6,967
5 Direct investment	26,222	29,050
6 Percent of rate of return	29.1	25.2
7 Reinvested earnings as a percent of adjusted earnings	45.9	17.2

Source: U.S. Department of Commerce, Bureau of Economic Analysis, *Selectected Data on U.S. Direct Investment Abroad, 1966–76*, (Washington, D.C.: Government Printing Office, 1977).

TABLE 5.8

U.S. Direct Investment, Net Flows of Capital and Income, Trinidad, 1966–76
($ million)

Year	Net Capital Flow (1)	Reinvested Earnings (2)	Receipts of Income (3)	Adjusted Earnings (4)	Direct Investment (5)	Rate of Return (4) ÷ (5) (6)	(2) as Percent of (4)
1966	12	3	12	15	207	7.2	20.0
1967	4	6	D	D	217	N.A.	N.A.
1968	–10	9	D	D	215	N.A.	N.A.
1969	D	D	D	D	185	N.A.	N.A.
1970	D	D	D	D	198	N.A.	N.A.
1971	67	–3	12	9	262	3.4	0.0
1972	19	*	14	14	280	5.0	0.0
1973	146	6	96	102	433	23.5	5.8
1974	72	14	164	178	549	32.4	7.8
1975	77	10	138	148	656	22.5	6.7
1976	55	5	100	105	715	14.6	4.7
1971–76	436	32	524	556			

D = suppressed to avoid disclosure of data of individual U.S. reporters.
* = less than $500,000.

Source: U.S. Department of Commerce, Bureau of Economic Analysis.

strategy, of course, has been greatly assisted by the sharp increase in the price of oil in 1973. As Jane Rothenberg and Amy Wishner put it:

> This strategy for development was based on oil money and the 1970's brought the government an unexpected boom. By 1970, a new oil discovery by Amoco had sent half a dozen consortia—composed of U.S. companies—scurrying for offshore exploration and exploitation rights. By 1971, Amoco predicted that oil from its new offshore find (immediately pumping 50,000 barrels per day and increasing Trinidad-Tobago's production by one-third) would be supplying 150,000 bpd by 1973 [*Miami Herald*, December 26, 1971].
>
> The real big money, however, was to come in 1973 when the so-called oil crises sent prices skyrocketing and companies off around the world in search of new sources of crude. In the years 1973 and 1974, total foreign investment in Trinidad-Tobago doubled, topping the one billion mark. Half of this investment was in oil and petrochemicals, mostly from U.S. companies. And this boom was not considered temporary. By 1975 the dismal forecast of shrinking oil reserves had given way to prediction that Trinidad's new off-shore reserves would last 20 years.[2]

THE COST OF TECHNOLOGY

In addition to the outflow of investment income to the United States is the outflow of payments in the form of royalties and fees for the transfer of technology. Table 5.11 shows that by far the largest flow of such payments over the period 1966–76 was from Jamaica—a total of $121 million, compared to $36 million for Trinidad and Tobago. A rough measure of the extent of Caribbean technological dependence on the United States may be made by comparing the total Jamaican payments of royalties and fees to the rest of the world with those paid to the United States for 1971–74. According to the *Economic and Social Survey* for 1974, Jamaica paid a total of $52.6 million in royalties and fees to the rest of the world. U.S. Department of Commerce figures in Table 5.11 indicate that the United States received $57 million for the same years. The discrepancy may be due to hidden costs and intracompany transfer payments. Whatever the reason for the discrepancy, it is clear that the United States is the major supplier of industrial technology to Jamaica. This, of course, stems from the fact that the United States is the largest foreign investor in Jamaica and that U.S. technology follows U.S. direct investment.

A SIMPLE DEBT MODEL

Since heavy borrowing by Jamaica and Guyana is a fairly recent phenomenon, it is reasonable to assume that debt-service payments will not decline in the near future. Indeed, if the 1970–75 rate of increase in the external debt is maintained, debt-service payments may grow large enough to offset

TABLE 5.9

U.S. Direct Investment, Net Flows of Capital and Income, Guyana, 1966–76
($ million)

Year	Net Capital Flow (1)	Reinvested Earnings (2)	Receipts of Income (3)	Adjusted Earnings (4)	Direct Investment (5)	Rate of Return (4) ÷ (5) (6)
1966	D	*	1	1	D	N.A.
1967	D	1	1	2	D	N.A.
1968	D	0	1	1	40	2.5
1969	0	0	2	2	40	5.0
1970	0	*	1	1	40	2.5
1971	−5	0	1	1	35	2.8
1972	1	*	3	3	36	8.3
1973	D	*	1	2	D	N.A.
1934	D	*	2	2	20	10.0
1975	1	*	*	*	22	N.A.
1976	*	0	0	*	21	N.A.
1969–76	− 19					

D = suppressed to avoid disclosure of data of individual U.S. reporters.
* = less than $500,000 (±).

Source: U.S. Department of Commerce, Bureau of Economic Analysis.

TABLE 5.10

U.S. Direct Investment, Net Flows of Capital and Income, Barbados, 1966–76
($ million)

Year	Net Capital Flow (1)	Reinvested Earnings (2)	Receipts of Income (3)	Adjusted Earnings (4)	Direct Investment (5)
1966	1	*	*	*	3
1967	*	*	*	*	3
1968	3	*	*	*	6
1969	*	*	*	*	6
1970	3	*	*	*	9
1971	3	1	1	1	12
1972	5	1	*	1	18
1973	2	*	1	1	20
1974	*	*	1	1	20
1975	– 3	2	1	3	19
1976	1	1	2	3	20
1971–76	11		6		

* = less than $500,000.

Source: U.S. Department of Commerce, Bureau of Economic Analysis.

TABLE 5.11

Royalties and Fees Paid to the United States, 1966–76
($ million)

Year	Jamaica	Trinidad and Tobago	Guyana	Barbados
1966	5	2	*	*
1967	6	4	*	*
1968	7	4	*	*
1969	9	2	1	*
1970	13	2	*	*
1971	15	3	*	*
1972	16	4	*	*
1973	13	2	*	*
1974	13	4	*	1
1975	15	4	*	1
1976	9	5	*	1

* = an amount between − $500,000 and + $500,000.
Source: U.S. Department of Commerce, Bureau of Economic Analysis.

completely the inflow of debt capital. At that point, the external debt will cease to grow. A simple example provided by Goran Ohlin will illustrate:

> Take a flow of 20 year loans at 4%. With straight-line depreciation, the debt will grow to ten times the level of new lending, and the carrying charge, i.e., the net outflow from the borrower, will after 20 years settle at 40%. For each new dollar lent, $1.40 will flow in the opposite direction. [3]

Ohlin points out that a softening of the repayment terms

> can only defer the decline of the net flow, and in the end it actually makes the decline more pronounced. . . . The net flow can be held positive only by a progressive increase in low loans. It is intuitively clear that, if the rate of growth of the total debt is higher than the rate of interest, the net flow will remain positive. [4]

A simple model used by Ohlin [5] and based on one developed by Avramovic et al [6] emphasizes the relationship between interest rates and the net flow of funds. Assume that investment requirements exceed domestic savings and that the resources to meet this gap are borrowed. In the following equation, the net flow of lending (N) is made a function of the average (a) and marginal (b) rates of saving when national income grows at a steady rate (r):

$$N(t) = a - be^{rt}$$

It follows that if the marginal rate of savings is constant and greater than the average rate, $N(t)$ will decline. Ohlin makes the further assumption that "when N turns negative, that is when the capacity to save exceeds investment requirements, the excess in domestic savings is employed for repayment of the foreign debt instead of being used to raise the rate of growth further."[7] If it is necessary to borrow for 30 years to finance long-term planning and if national income is expected to grow at 3 percent a year, the number of years necessary for repayment after the termination of borrowing at various interest rates is shown as follows:

Interest Rates (percent)	Repayment Period (years)
5	∞
4	66
3	52
2	33

At the 5 percent rate of interest, the debt would never be repaid, despite the large reflow from borrower to lender. The lower the interest rate, the shorter the repayment period. At the critical interest rate of 4 percent, the debt reaches a maximum and turns down. At the end of the 66-year repayment period, the reflow would be 2.8 times as much as the maximum outflow at the beginning of the 96-year period.* The first third of the 96-year debt cycle will be one of inflow, while the last two-thirds will be one of outflow. Figure 5.1 illustrates this.

U.S. SHARE OF THE PUBLIC DEBT

The U.S. dollar component of Jamaica's gross national debt grew from 13.4 percent as of December 1970 to 33 percent as of May 1976. Equally dramatic was the growth of the gross external debt over the same period,[8] from 35.6 percent to 83.4 percent. As of May 1976, loans raised on the U.S. market and from the U.S. Agency for International Development (AID) accounted for 86 percent of the U.S. dollar debt with the rest composed primarily of loans from international institutions such as the World Bank and the Inter-American Development Bank (IDB). Lines of credit from commercial institutions were the largest single source of the U.S. dollar debt, comprising approximately 69 percent. Tables 5.12 and 5.13 show the distribution of the gross national debt and the gross external debt by currency of repayment.

---

*Thirty years of borrowing plus the repayment period of 66 years.

FIGURE 5.1

Relationship between Debt and Net Flow of Lending

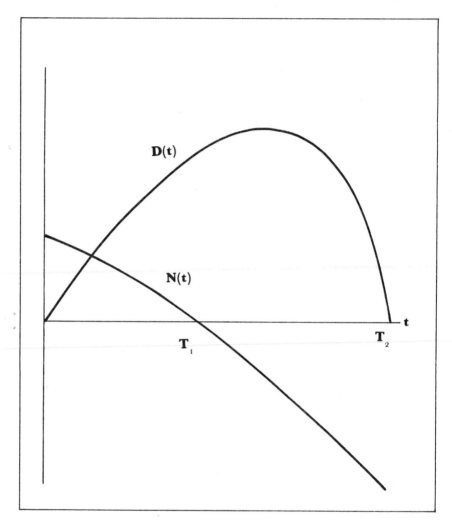

D = debt
N = net flow of lending
  t = time period

At the time when the net flow (N) changes direction, the debt (D) will still be growing by the interest accruing, that is, at a rate equal to the rate of interest. If the rate of interest is below a certain critical level, the debt will then reach a maximum and turn down.

Source: Goran Ohlin, *Aid and Indebtness* (Paris: Organisation for Economic Co-Operation and Development, 1966), p. 24.

TABLE 5.12

Distribution of Gross National Debt by Currency of Repayment
(J $ million)

Currency	As of December 31, 1970	Percent	As of May 1976	Percent
Jamaican dollars	172.1	62.5	610.2	60.4
Sterling	58.8	21.3	50.3	5.0
U.S. dollars	36.8	13.4	333.3	33.0
Canadian dollars	7.6	2.8	16.0	1.6
Gross national debt	275.3	100.0	1,009.8	100.0

Source: Bank of Jamaica, *Report and Statement of Accounts for* the Year Ended 31st December 1971; Bank of Jamaica, *Statistical Digest*, December 1976.

TABLE 5.13

Percentage Distribution of Gross External Debt of Jamaica by Currency of Repayment as of December 31, 1970–75

Year[a]	Sterling	U.S. Dollars	Canadian Dollars
1970	57.0	35.6	7.4
1971	53.3	41.4	5.3
1972	46.6	47.4	6.0
1973	31.8	60.9	7.3
1974	21.5	72.9	5.6
1975	15.0	80.9	4.1
1976[b]	12.6	83.4	4.0

[a]The total for each year adds up to 100.0 percent.
[b]As of the end of May.
Source: *Economic and Social Survey Jamaica 1975* (Kingston: The Government Printer, 1976); Bank of Jamaica, *Statistical Digest*.

Since the early 1970s, the figures clearly show that the composition of foreign capital flows into Jamaica has changed drastically. In 1970, direct investment accounted for all of the long-term capital inflow; in 1976, it was completely replaced by government borrowing. During the 1960s and early 1970s, the major share of direct investment was undertaken by U.S. firms in the bauxite and tourist industries. In the latter part of the 1970s, the U.S. government and U.S. private financial institutions are the major suppliers of foreign debt capital. This transformation has made Jamaica far more dependent on the United States in the 1970s than it was in the 1960s. The primary reason for this greater dependence lies in the fact that the change in the composition of capital flows has rendered Jamaican fiscal policy helpless to influence those flows. Ironically, this change has wrested out of the hands of Jamaica the influence over economic decision making which is the objective of its strategy of ownership and control. The general problem is described succinctly by Harry Johnson:

> Foreign official capital is obtained by governmental negotiation and is not a variable controlled by fiscal policy as such; rather, the general conduct of fiscal policy is constrained by the terms imposed by the official suppliers of foreign capital as a condition of development assistance, while fiscal policy must aim to make effective use of the extra resources provided by foreign financial assistance and to provide for interest and amortization payments on it. Private foreign capital, on the other hand, is a variable subject to direct influence by fiscal policy in three major ways: through the influence of the tariff structure (and other barriers to trade) in creating an incentive for foreign enterprises to establish productive facilities in the country rather than export to it; through the influence of the general system of corporate income taxation, special investment incentives and subsidies, and so forth on the private return to investment; and through the influence of special incentives or disincentives to the investment of foreign, as contrasted with domestic, capital. [9]

Not only has fiscal policy lost its potency but it has come to be dictated by the International Monetary Fund. A prime condition of the IMF soft loan negotiated by Jamaica in May 1978 was that a new tax program be implemented to eliminate the budget deficit. This external control of Jamaica's fiscal policy represents a degree of dependence that surpasses that of colonial times.

What emerges from all this is the stark reality that U.S. foreign capital, whether portfolio or direct, is vital to the survival of Caribbean economies. The composition and source of that capital may change due to the new strategy of ownership and control or to domestic mismanagement, but the dependence remains. Manley's declaration that foreign capital will become more "public and institutional" was meant to imply that capital in this form would change the character of dependence through economic diversification and collective self-reliance. Under traditional forms of direct private foreign investment, dependence has been viewed as cumulative, [10] that is, the small open developing economy becomes progressively hooked into the metropolitan economy. A prime example, of course, is the relationship between Puerto Rico and the United States.

Whatever the character of foreign capital, if it is used to finance programs that do not expand productive capacity, the goals of economic diversification and collective self-reliance invariably founder on a stagnant indigenous productive capacity.

Unlike profits, debt payments are not a function of economic condition: they are fixed. Thus the burden of the debt increases when economic growth lags. The situation becomes cumulative as the country becomes more indebted; drastic measures to ration the use of foreign exchange lead to further borrowing to meet debt-service charges. Lagging economic growth combined with social and political developments induce additional outflows of capital, both financial and human, to further offset financial capital inflows from abroad.

Human capital outflow in the form of the migration of skilled workers from the Caribbean to the United States became significant in the latter part of the 1960s, although unfortunately this is reflected only in a marginal way in the balance of payments under the item of foreign travel. This migration of human resources will be examined in Chapter 6.

NOTES

1. See, for example, Claremont Kirton, "A Preliminary Analysis of Imperial Penetration and Control via the Foreign Debt: A Study of Jamaica" *Essays on Power and Change in Jamaica*, ed. Carl Stone and Aggrey Brown (Kingston: Jamaica Publishing House, 1977), pp. 72–88.

2. Jane Rothenberg and Amy Wishner, "Focus on Trinidad," *NACLA's Latin America & Empire Report* 10 (1976): 28.

3. Goran Ohlin, *Aid and Indebtedness* (Paris: Organisation for Economic Co-operation and Development, 1966), p. 11.

4. Ibid., p. 13.

5. Ibid., pp. 23–26.

6. Dragoslav Avramovic and Associates, *Economic Growth and External Debt* (Baltimore: Johns Hopkins University Press, 1964).

7. Ohlin, op. cit.

8. Kirton (op. cit., pp. 73–74) argues that the published data on Jamaica's foreign debt understates and obscures the magnitude of government's indebtedness to foreign sources of finance:

> Firstly, the foreign debt statistics do not incorporate overseas debts incurred by quasi-government institutions, which debts are guaranteed by the government. Furthermore, the data fail to record the country's obligations to the International Monetary Fund (IMF) as part of the foreign debt . . .
>
> Secondly, foreign debt statistics record only those debts which are denominated in foreign currency, regardless of the nature of the ownership of the lender. This means, therefore, that when a foreign-owned institution operating locally lends Jamaican dollars to the government, their debt is recorded as part of the country's internal debt despite the obvious implications of foreign ownership, which include transfer of profit overseas . . .
>
> Thirdly, some government sources have implied that short-term loans are not included as part of the foreign debt because these loans are usually of a self-liquidating nature.

Kirton also argues that debt charges are understated to the extent that they do not include management charges, finders' fees, and advertising expenses incurred by government when market issues are made in foreign countries, the statutory sinking fund provision which represents amounts put aside for the redemption of securities when payment becomes due, and the exemption of foreign lenders from a 12.5 percent withholding tax which is usually paid on interest earnings transferred overseas by foreign agencies. The withholding exemption operates as an incentive to the foreign lender, which effectively increases the rate of interest on borrowed funds.

9. Harry G. Johnson, "Fiscal Policy and the Balance of Payments," in *Government Finance and Economic Development*, ed. Alan T. Peacock and Gerald Hauser (Paris: Organisation for Economic Co-operation and Development, 1965), p. 158.

10. Eric Williams, *From Columbus to Castro: The History of the Caribbean 1492–1969* (London: Andre Deutsch, 1970), p. 510.

6

Migration of Human Resources To the United States

MIGRATION AS AN ESCAPE VALVE

George Roberts points out that over the 14-year period between 1946 and 1960, all the West Indian islands, with the exception of Trinidad, experienced substantial reductions in the natural increase of their populations as a result of emigration.[1] "In the Windwards between 48 percent and 38 percent of their natural increase has been cut as a result of emigration. In St. Kitts the proportion was 53 percent, in Antigua 36 percent, in Barbados 33 percent and in Jamaica 35 percent."[2] The smallest island in the group, Montserrat, annually lost more than twice its natural increase to the exodus to the United Kingdom.

Trinidad, according to Roberts,

> presents the outstanding exception, having received an annual increment of nearly 3 percent of its natural increase as a result of emigration. This does not mean that this island has not shared in the movement to the United Kingdom. It probably signifies that this movement has been considerably overshadowed by the traditional influx from the neighboring islands, which, despite prevailing restrictions, has continued.[3]

Roberts indicates that the net outflow of immigrants between 1943 and 1960 from Jamaica alone was 195,700, and the rate of emigration from the metropolitan parish of Kingston was a high 32 percent.[4]

Dependence on an escape valve to moderate the rate of population growth in the West Indies has permeated most of the literature on Caribbean population growth. In the aftermath of the 1962 ban on West Indian migration to the United Kingdom, George Abbott speculated about alternatives: "If mounting population pressures operate to open up alternative avenues of outlet after 1965, we can visualize the volume of migration taking place at the end of the sixties and the early seventies as comparable to that of the late fifties, just before the ban was imposed."[5]

Roberts also saw alternative outlets as an indispensable feature of West Indian population policy:

> It seems therefore that emigration to the United Kingdom constituting a powerful curb on population growth has come to be accepted by the West Indian Governments, who, having realized its immediate advantages are prepared to do everything within their power to maintain it. It may thus be construed as one leg of a population policy for the region. Doubtless it may be possible to extract from other countries, especially the United States of America and Canada, rights of entry . . . which would constitute a further curb on population growth.[6]

Like the mass emigration of Puerto Ricans to the mainland United States in the 1950s, the mass emigration of West Indians to the United Kingdom about the same time allowed the Caribbean to export its unemployment to the metropolitan centers. There was no process of selection of the emigrants since they were either U.S. citizens (in the case of Puerto Rico) or British citizens (in the case of the Commonwealth Caribbean). Thus the official encouragement of migration to the United Kingdom was not only an explicit population strategy but an implicit employment strategy as well.

The liberalization of U.S. immigration policy in 1965 sharply increased the volume of Caribbean migration to the United States. Sonia Sinclair sees this movement as vital to Jamaica:

> Without this emigration very rapid increments to the population will materialize. . . . It seems to be the only means of controlling the population growth in the short term. Its continuance is highly desirable if massive increments to the population are to be avoided. . . . With the present age structure considerable increases must take place up to the end of the century, unless very appreciable emigration can be counted on. In the absence of this, growth of a high order will be experienced up to the end of the century regardless of what reductions in levels of fertility are achieved.[7]

THE NEW U.S. IMMIGRATION POLICY

In the early years after Jamaica and Trinidad and Tobago became independent, migration to the United States changed very little. The U.S. Immigration Act of 1965 removed the national origins quota and granted Western Hemisphere countries—including the West Indies—nonquota status. The new immigration policy which this act promulgated had two basic objectives: the reuniting of families; and the admission of workers needed in the U.S.

economy. It also coincided with a sharp decline in unemployment rates in the United States. With the rapid expansion of the service sector in the United States, the full employment situation of the 1960s left a wide range of skilled as well as unskilled jobs unfilled. Thus the number of immigrant visas that were issued to West Indians following the Immigration Act of 1965 increased sharply. After a three-year transition, a quota of 120,000 visas per year for the Western Hemisphere was put into effect in 1968. But there was no preference system governing the selection process as there was for the Eastern Hemisphere. Franklin Abrams describes the situation this way:

> Since the original preference proposals had been drawn up with no numerical limit for Western Hemisphere immigration and since in any case the supply of visas was expected to exceed the demand, no attempt was made in the 1965 Act to give relatives preference over workers, or to distinguish between closer and more distant relatives or between workers of varying levels of skills. Applicants were simply granted visas on a first-come, first-served basis. However, in order "to protect the American economy from job competition and from adverse working standards as a consequence of immigrant workers entering the labor market," labor certification was required of all immigrants entering the labor market except for parents, children under 21, or spouses of citizens or permanent resident aliens. [8]

In general, the labor certification program is regarded as a failure because most immigrants arrive as relatives exempt from the certification requirements. [9] According to Abrams, the reforms introduced by the 1965 act for the Western Hemisphere contributed to an increase in illegal immigration, a slight downgrading of the average skill of arriving immigrants, and the creation of a two-and-one-half-year backlog of would-be immigrants. [10] These unexpected problems led the United States to pass the Western Hemisphere Bill in September 1976 which equalized the treatment of Eastern and Western Hemisphere immigrants in the following ways:

It maintained the Western Hemisphere quota of 120,000 exclusive of immediate relatives of U.S. citizens.

It raised the quota for an individual colony or dependency from 200 to 600.

It imposed a quota of 20,000 per country per year under the overall quota of 120,000 for the Western Hemisphere.

It terminated the practice of charging the adjustment of Cuban refugees to permanent resident status against the 120,000 Western Hemisphere quota.

It applied to the Western Hemisphere the same preference system used for granting visas to immigrants from the Eastern Hemisphere.

The large pool of potential emigrants in the Caribbean has made it easy for the United States to draw on that labor to fill positions in the United States as the need arises. In addition, the adaptability of the West Indian worker to production processes in an industrial economy assures potential employers that a high level of productivity will be maintained. This latter point is underscored by Robert Aronson in his study of bauxite workers in Jamaica: "The Jamaican worker is culturally receptive to employment in a modern industrial enterprise. Even though the tools of an advanced industrial economy do not exist to a large extent in Jamaica, especially in the rural sector, certain cultural barriers to industrialization also do not exist."[11]

POSTINDEPENDENCE MIGRATION TO THE UNITED STATES

Over the years 1962 to 1976, 245,400 immigrants from Jamaica, Trinidad and Tobago, Guyana, and Barbados were admitted to the United States (see Table 6.1). This represents roughly 6 percent of the total population of these countries in 1975, and 17 percent of the natural increase in their population (see Tables 6.2 to 6.5). Overall net emigration to the rest of the world from the four

TABLE 6.1

Caribbean Migration to the United States, 1962–76

Year	Jamaica	Trinidad and Tobago	Barbados	Guyana	Total
1962	1,573	388	406	268	2,635
1963	1,880	448	376	273	2,977
1964	1,762	413	393	296	2,864
1965	1,837	485	406	233	2,961
1966	2,743	756	520	377	4,396
1967	10,483	2,160	1,037	857	14,537
1968	17,470	5,266	2,024	1,148	25,908
1969	16,947	6,835	1,957	1,615	27,354
1970	15,033	7,350	1,774	1,763	25,920
1971	14,571	7,130	1,731	2,115	25,647
1972	13,427	6,615	1,620	2,826	24,488
1973	9,963	7,035	1,448	2,969	21,415
1974	12,408	6,516	1,461	3,241	23,526
1975	11,076	5,982	1,618	3,169	21,845
1976	9,026	4,839	1,743	3,326	18,934
Total	140,199	62,218	18,514	24,476	245,407

Note: All figures are by country of birth and are for fiscal years ending June 30.
Source: U.S. Immigration and Naturalization Service, *Annual Reports.*

TABLE 6.2

Natural Increase in Population, 1962–75

Year	Jamaica	Trinidad and Tobago	Guyana	Barbados
1962	52,104	27,735	19,620	4,765
1963	51,518	26,428	19,393	4,793
1964	55,790	26,345	18,767	4,379
1965	55,684	25,222	18,130	4,453
1966	57,076	23,019	20,119	4,307
1967	54,143	21,687	18,848	3,408
1968	50,845	20,991	19,464	3,429
1969	50,574	18,062	18,095	3,221
1970	50,023	18,195	19,186	2,819
1971	52,199	19,072	19,930	3,138
1972	52,249	21,094	20,961	3,258
1973	47,700	18,714	21,461	2,797
1974	47,100	19,422	21,656	2,744
1975	47,400	18,056	21,823	2,687

Sources: Jamaica: *Demographic Statistics* (Kingston: Department of Statistics, 1976); Trinidad: *Annual Statistical Digest* (Port-of-Spain: Central Statistical Office); Guyana: *Annual Statistical Abstract* (Georgetown: Ministry of Economic Development); Barbados: *Monthly Digest of Statistics* (Bridgetown: Statistical Service), *Economic Survey 1968; 1971* (Bridgetown: Economic Planning Unit, 1969; 1972).

countries reduced the natural increase in their combined population by 32.3 percent, with migration to the United States accounting for roughly half of the net effect of migration on population growth. Table 6.4 shows that for individual countries over the 14-year period 1962–75, net emigration reduced the natural increase in population by 36.9 percent for Jamaica, 34.4 percent for Trinidad and Tobago, 25.5 percent for Guyana, and 4.9 percent for Barbados. Thus the role of emigration in reducing the pressure of population on economic opportunities was apparently greater for Jamaica, Trinidad and Tobago, and Guyana than it was for Barbados. Yet as Table 6.5 shows, migration from Barbados to the United States represented one-third of the natural increase in its population for the 14-year period. The figures in Table 6.4 suggest that in the first half of the 1970s, migration to Barbados may have offset the outflow to the United States.[12]

Migration to the United States from all four countries began to accelerate in 1967, two years after the U.S. Immigration Act of 1965, and a year after all the

TABLE 6.3

Net Emigration, 1962–75

Year	Jamaica	Trinidad and Tobago	Guyana	Barbados
1962	−25,704	+ 2,600	− 5,514	−1,345
1963	−15,118	+ 2,322	− 2,631	−1,701
1964	−13,290	− 2,116	− 4,246	− 551
1965	−10,084	− 3,050	− 2,036	−2,155
1966	−17,376	− 5,140	− 835	−1,159
1967	−30,943	− 8,860	− 2,394	− 952
1968	−31,045	− 9,060	− 2,608	−1,155
1969	−26,074	−15,600	− 5,888	−2,512
1970	−24,723	−17,370	− 6,546	+ 165
1971	−20,199	− 7,530	− 2,930	− 445
1972	−20,949	− 7,030	− 2,961	+1,442
1973	− 8,100	− 9,620	− 3,461	+ 203
1974	−11,100	− 6.662	−14,656	+3,756
1975	−12,700	− 6,000	−15,823	+1,113
Total	−267,405	−93,116	−72,529	−5,296

Note: Net emigration is the difference between the change in the population and the natural increase in the population. The figures include temporary as well as permanent migration flows.

Sources: Jamaica: *Demographic Statistics* (Kingston: Department of Statistics, 1976); Trinidad: *Annual Statistical Digest* (Port-of-Spain: Central Statistical Office); Guyana: *Annual Statistical Abstract* (Georgetown: Ministry of Economic Development); Barbados: *Monthly Digest of Statistics* (Bridgetown: Statistical Service), *Economic Survey 1968; 1971* (Bridgetown: Economic Planning Unit, 1969; 1972).

countries had gained their political independence from Great Britain.* Clearly, the nonquota status which the act conferred upon them and the priority which it gave to the reuniting of families dramatically increased the number of immigrants to the United States.

Those who emigrated were uncertain about the economic vitality of their small countries; they had taken seriously the widely publicized claims of the U.S.

---

* Jamaica and Trinidad and Tobago became independent in 1962, and Barbados and Guyana in 1966.

policy makers that economic policy instruments were refined enough to tune out serious fluctuations from future U.S. economic growth. Thus Caribbean immigrants left the uncertainty of their own condition behind for the certainty of economic prosperity in a country which was experiencing record low unemployment rates. Of the 245,400 who migrated to the United States between 1962 and 1976, 229,000 (93 percent) did so between 1967 and 1976. Approximately 53 percent of them were classified as workers and the rest as "housewives, children and others with no occupation or occupation not reported" (see Table 6.6). Although this latter group is generally regarded as "dependents," many of them seek employment immediately upon their arrival in the United States.

Of those classified as workers, five groups stand out numerically: professional, technical, and kindred workers (**PTK**); clerical and kindred workers; craftsmen, foremen, and kindred workers; operatives and kindred workers; and private household workers. Women are heavily represented in the PTK category as nurses and school teachers. The same is true of clerical and kindred workers. The category of private household workers is almost exclusively women. As we

TABLE 6.4

Net Emigration as a Percent of the Natural Increase in the Population, 1962–75

Year	Jamaica	Trinidad and Tobago	Guyana	Barbados
1962	−49.3	+ 9.3	−28.1	−28.2
1963	−29.3	+ 8.8	−13.5	−35.5
1964	−23.8	− 8.0	−22.6	−12.6
1965	−18.1	−12.0	−11.2	−48.4
1966	−30.4	−22.3	− 4.1	−26.9
1967	−57.1	−40.8	−12.7	−27.9
1968	−61.0	−43.1	−13.4	−33.6
1969	−52.5	−86.3	−32.5	−78.0
1970	−49.4	−95.5	−34.1	+ 5.8
1971	−38.6	−39.5	−14.7	−14.2
1972	−40.0	−33.3	−14.1	+44.2
1973	−16.9	−51.4	−16.1	+ 7.2
1974	−23.5	−34.3	−67.6	+136.8
1975	−26.8	−33.2	−72.5	+41.4
Average	−36.9	−34.4	−25.5	− 4.9

Source: Calculated from Tables 6.2 and 6.3.

TABLE 6.5

Migration to the United States as a Percent of the Natural Increase in Population, 1962–75

Year	Jamaica	Trinidad	Guyana	Barbados
1962	3.0	1.4	1.3	8.5
1963	3.6	1.7	1.4	7.8
1964	3.1	1.5	1.6	8.9
1965	3.3	1.9	1.3	9.1
1966	4.8	3.3	1.8	12.0
1967	19.3	9.9	4.5	30.4
1968	34.3	25.0	5.9	59.0
1969	33.5	37.8	8.9	60.7
1970	30.0	40.4	9.2	62.9
1971	27.9	37.4	10.6	55.1
1972	25.7	31.3	13.5	49.7
1973	20.8	33.5	13.8	51.7
1974	26.3	34.9	14.9	53.2
1975	23.4	33.1	14.5	60.2
Average	18.5	20.9	7.4	37.8

Source: Calculated from Tables 6.1 and 6.2.

would expect, the categories of craftsmen and operatives are dominated by men.*

The first four categories are crucial in terms of the loss of skilled workers, since they represent people with years of formal and on-the-job training, a cost borne by the sending country. This export of human capital from poor countries to a rich country is a manifestation of the interconnected character of the world capitalist system. Skilled workers who are underutilized in the peripheral hinterland of the system are attracted to those central areas which promise greater economic opportunities. Thus while capital moves from the center to the periphery to generate perpetual flows of profits and interest back to the center, labor moves to the center to occupy positions in the expanding service sector. By U.S. standards, these positions are not generally high-paying, yet they are substantially higher than wage levels in the immigrants' home country.

---

* In October 1976, women in the Jamaican labor force accounted for 54 percent of the professional, technical, and managerial occupations; 63.3 percent of the clerical and service occupations; and 13.3 percent of the craftsmen, production process, and operative occupations.

The extent to which emigration has affected the growth of skilled manpower may be illustrated with the case of Jamaica for the years 1973–74 (see Table 6.7). The highest rate of emigration is clearly from the incremental output of medical doctors, followed by accountants, engineers, and nurses. However, we can assume that in the period of peak emigration to the United States, 1967–69, when the average annual emigration of engineers and nurses exceeded 50 and 600, respectively, the rates of emigration were much higher than those indicated in Table 6.7.

In the years 1962–76, 7,700 persons in medical and related fields in the four countries migrated to the United States. As Table 6.8 details, nurses easily

TABLE 6.6

Occupational Distribution of Caribbean Migration to the United States, Totals for 1967–76

Occupational Group	Jamaica	Trinidad	Guyana*	Barbados	Total
Professional, technical, and kindred workers	9,906	4,011	2,325	1,407	17,649
Farmers and farm managers	232	10	20	4	266
Managers, officials, and Proprietors	1,771	871	441	221	3,304
Clerical and kindred	8,449	4,329	2,143	1,191	16,112
Sales workers	1,089	480	192	176	1,937
Craftsmen, foremen, and kindred	11,054	5,442	1,587	1,518	19,601
Operatives and kindred	8,727	3,451	1,141	1,090	14,409
Private household workers	23,088	7,026	1,578	2,827	34,519
Service workers except private household	5,422	2,621	834	992	9,869
Farm laborers and foremen	976	50	51	69	1,146
Laborers, except farm and mine	1,268	513	125	243	2,149
Housewives, children, and others with no occupations or occupations not reported	58,422	30,924	11,735	6,675	107,756
Total	130,404	59,728	22,172	16,413	228,717

*Figures are for 1968–76.
Source: U.S. Immigration and Naturalization Service, *Annual Reports*.

TABLE 6.7

Average Annual Increase of Skilled Manpower and Migration in Selected Occupations in Jamaica, 1973–74

Occupation	Gross Increase	Emigration	Net Increase	Emigration as a percent of Gross Increase
Medical doctors	47	19	28	40.4
Nurses	463	110	353	23.8
Teachers and other instructors	1,155	56	1,099	4.8
Engineers	90	24	66	26.7
Accountants	191	52	139	27.2

Note: Skilled manpower includes those who were trained abroad.

Source: U.S. Department of Justice, Immigration and Naturalization Service; *Economic and Social Survey Jamaica 1974* (Kingston: The Government Printer, 1975).

dominate the flow, accounting for over 77 percent. More than half of the total Caribbean medical emigration came from Jamaica.

Table 6.9 shows that annual migration from the PTK and management group represented roughly 10 percent of the incremental growth of manpower for that group. Thus the growth of the PTK group, though positive, was reduced by emigration. For the group of craftsmen, production process, and kindred workers, incremental growth was negative for the three-year period suggesting that emigration and attrition far outstripped additions to that group.

The migration of skilled manpower has aggravated labor shortages in a number of areas of economic activity. Some indication of this is given by the number of work permits held by non-Jamaicans. In 1974, for example, when the output of PTK and managerial manpower was 2,881, 743 emigrated and 2,838 non-Jamaicans held work permits in various professional and skilled occupations, including medical and related fields.

In its Third Five Year Plan 1969–73, Trinidad recognized the migration of skilled manpower as a threat to its development effort:

This loss of skilled manpower must be stemmed if our investments in Education and Training are to bear returns. It is also quite obvious that our development effort will flounder without trained nationals. Trained persons in both the public and private sectors will have to be inspired with a greater sense of commitment to enable them to resist tempting offers of overseas jobs.[13]

This loss is particularly critical for a development strategy which seeks to achieve greater local control over private-sector economic decision-making processes.

DOMESTIC UNEMPLOYMENT AND MIGRATION

Widespread unemployment exists side by side with chronic labor shortages in certain areas of economic activity in the Caribbean. In general, the shortages occur in occupations at the upper end of the skill spectrum, while the surplus labor (and the unemployment) occurs at the lower end. The slow expansion of economic opportunities in the semiskilled and unskilled occupations has not made it possible for the economy to absorb a large percentage of the semiskilled and unskilled labor force, let alone the annual increment to the labor force in those areas. Unemployment wastes resources, human or otherwise. If, by some magic, all unemployed human resources were to migrate to some other country where they became real rather than potential resources, production in the sending country would not be affected. In fact, per capita consumption would tend to rise. The concern with the migration of human resources has not been with the loss of unemployed semiskilled and unskilled labor. Rather it has been

TABLE 6.8

Migration of Professional and Technical Workers in Medical and Related Fields to the United States, 1962-76

Occupational Group	Jamaica	Trinidad and Tobago	Barbados	Guyana	Total
Nurses	3,310	1,238	446	967	5,961
Physicians, surgeons, and dentists	344	130	35	93	602
Dietitians and nutritionists	108	43	26	33	210
Optometrists	3	4	1	0	8
Medical and dental technicians	370	206	72	80	728
Therapists and healers	24	14	4	9	51
Pharmacists	63	24	8	14	109
Veterinarians	14	7	2	7	30
Total	4,236	1,666	594	1,203	7,699

Source: U.S. Department of Justice, Immigration and Naturalization Service.

TABLE 6.9

Annual Incremental Growth of Selected Occupational Groups in Jamaica, 1974–76

Occupational Groups	1974	1975	1976
	Incremental Growth		
Professional, technical, administrative, executive, managerial, and related occupations	5,500*	12,800*	1,900*
Craftsmen, production process, and operating occupations	1,750*	−5,150*	−1,350*
	Migration		
Professional, technical, administrative, executive, managerial, and related occupations	743	694	715
Craftsmen, production process, and operating occupations	1,044	929	1,342

*Figures for each year represent the average of the figures for April and October.

Sources: Jamaica Department of Statistics, *The Labour Force*, 1976, U.S. Department of Justice, Immigration and Naturalization Service *Annual Reports*.

with the loss of highly skilled labor that is generally in short supply. But even skilled labor in many areas is underutilized. The question is how much of a resource is labor, skilled or unskilled, if it is unemployed or underemployed? If we define resource as a means of supplying want, then the large army of the unemployed is merely standing by waiting to be converted into productive resources. Thus the investment in their education becomes an investment in future social dislocation. As Carl Stone sees it,

> the vicious circle of joblessness (out of which education is less and less an escape route) means that try as we may to raise educational levels, the motivation to learn is going to drop even further below the existing very unsatisfactory levels. No fancy curriculum changes or teaching methods are going to make any difference. Youth without hope of jobs are going to be even more uninterested than they are at the moment in either vocational or academic pursuits. Pious clichés about the great value of our human resources mean absolutely nothing

TABLE 6.10

Labor Force and Unemployment by Age Groups in Jamaica for Selected Years

Year*	14-19	20-24	25-34	35-44	45-54	55-64	65 and Over	Total
1968								
Share of labor force	27.5		20.5	19.0	16.8	10.5	5.7	100.0
Unemployment rate	34.9		21.0	17.2	7.0	5.9	2.0	18.5
1974								
Share of labor force	13.3	14.2	21.5	17.9	15.4	10.9	6.8	100.0
Unemployment rate	44.2	30.6	19.0	16.9	11.7	10.3	6.6	20.7
1975								
Share of labor force	13.3	14.4	21.9	17.1	15.4	10.6	7.2	100.0
Unemployment rate	45.9	30.4	19.4	15.0	13.5	10.4	6.7	21.0
1976								
Share of labor force	12.8	15.2	22.3	16.7	14.9	11.1	6.9	100.0
Unemployment rate	54.3	37.5	22.7	17.1	13.2	7.7	11.2	24.2

*Figures are for October of each year.

Source: Jamaica Department of Statistics, *The Labour Force 1976*.

unless we provide the material motivation for youth to learn and develop skills. What future can any country have if its youth become demoralized by hopelessness? The only beneficiaries are going to be the subcultures of crime, violence, idleness and indiscipline. The growing signs of this trend are already very evident.[14]

A vivid picture of this problem emerges in Table 6.10. Between 1968 and 1976, the labor force grew younger, with the share of those under 35 growing from 48.0 to 50.3 percent. During the same period, the unemployment rate for this group grew from 34.9 to 44.2 percent. Thus as the labor force became progressively younger, it also became progressively unemployed. Work experience is becoming a rarity for a larger share of the growing army of the unemployed. In October 1976, 60 percent of those unemployed had not worked in the previous 12 months, and 28 percent had never worked. Most of these people are likely to be the younger members of the work force, since the incidence of unemployment is greatest among them.

The accelerated increase in emigration to the United States and Canada in recent years of those in the age groups below 29 may have moderated—even if slightly—the unemployment pressure generated by new entrants into the labor force. Most of these emigrants have benefited from the preference given to relatives under U.S. immigration law and therefore need not have a skill or satisfy any work certification requirements. Thus the push effect of chronic unemployment conditions is facilitated by a U.S. immigration policy which has the reuniting of families as one of its principal goals.

TEMPORARY MIGRATION

In addition to permanent migration, there is temporary migration (under contractual arrangements) of farm workers—mostly from Jamaica—to the United States. Table 6.11 shows that between 10,000 and 15,000 Caribbean workers are recruited each year for work on U.S. farms. Most of them come from Jamaica, and most of them go to Florida to reap sugar cane. Labor contracts are negotiated between Caribbean governments and U.S. sugar growers. In the negotiations, Caribbean governments are represented by the British West Indies Central Labor Organization (BWICLO), which has offices in the United States. The sugar cane growers are represented by the Florida Sugar Producers Association and the Florida Fruit and Vegetable Association. About two-thirds of the farm workers are hired by three companies: the U.S. Sugar Company, the Okeelanta Sugar Division of the Gulf & Western Food Products Company, and the Sugar Cane Growers Cooperative of Florida.[15]

According to the North American Congress on Latin America (NACLA), "West Indians are no longer the emergency supplemental work force that the U.S. government first imported during World War II. Rather they have become a regular part of the farm labor force of the United States."[16] American growers

TABLE 6.11

Flow of West Indian Farm Workers to the United States, 1963–76

Year	Total Workers	Jamaica	Number of Workers Going to Florida
1963	15,937	9,373	12,727
1964	16,841	11,542	13,020
1965	15,265	9,161	13,099
1966	10,135	9,907	8,762
1967	11,401	12,085	9,056
1968	10,602	9,464	8,711
1969	10,909	12,028	8,230
1970	11,887	13,839	9,319
1971	12,244	10,808	9,050
1972	11,425	10,118	8,276
1973	12,837	10,743	8,639
1974	12,582	10,042	8,224
1975	12,813	10,262	8,427
1976	10,958	8,656	8,052

Sources: Total workers and workers going to Florida taken from "Caribbean Migration: Contract Labor in U.S. Agriculture," *NACLA Report on the Americas* 11 (1977). Jamaica figures from *Economic Survey Jamaica*. In 1967, 1969, and 1970, the number of Jamaican farm workers is shown to be larger than the total number of farm workers for those years. This discrepancy may be attributed to the fact that the data were taken from two different sources.

prefer to use West Indians for two reasons: under the provisions of the labor contract, they can get more work out of these imported cane cutters for a given wage rate, thereby reducing the cost of labor; and growers have more control over the farm workers. The threat of immediate repatriation (provided in the contract) effectively eliminates any disruptive activity or any attempt to become involved in union activity and assures the growers maximum output per man.[17]

The effect of this program is likely to be a reduction of the unemployment pressure at home as well as an increase in foreign exchange for Jamaica. Under the contractual arrangements, compulsory savings amounting to 16 percent of the farm worker's wages are deducted by the U.S. employers and remitted to the Agricultural Workers Bank in Jamaica. Table 6.12 shows farm worker remittances from 1971–76.

TABLE 6.12

Remittances from Abroad by Individuals to Jamaica 1971–76
(J $ thousand)

Item	1971	1972	1973	1974	1975	1976
U.K. postal and money orders	9,138	11,537	15,654	14,722	15,711	9,039
U.S. money orders	2,415	2,202	2,016	1,863	1,801	1,492
Canadian money orders	330	335	383	420	356	372
B.W.I. money orders	159	12	2	1	2	3
Total postal and money orders	12,042	14,086	18,055	16,511	17,870	10,906
Farm worker remittances	1,785	1,868	3,204	3,116	4,247	4,307
Remittances through government savings banks	341	284	N.A.	N.A.	N.A.	N.A.
Remittances through commercial banks	17,680	25,600	28,150	29,442	25,109	30,000
Total Remittances	31,848	41,838	49,409	49,069	47,226	45,213
Net investment income outflow	87,500	100,600	52,800	61,500	93,500	103,000

Note: The figures on remittances from abroad present a partial picture of the remittances coming from the United States. U.S. money orders and farm worker remittances have averaged about 12 percent of total remittances. The largest share of remittance is made through commercial banks, but the Bank of Jamaica does not publish a breakdown of the sources of these remittances. Such a breakdown would probably show that a major share of total remittances comes from the United States.

Source: Jamaica *Statistical Abstracts*, 1972–76.

REMITTANCES FROM ABROAD

Remittances from abroad are frequently cited as one of the major benefits of migration for the sending countries. The figures in Table 6.12 show that for Jamaica these remittances averaged (J) $44 million a year, reaching a peak of (J) $49.4 million in 1973. This is not an inconsequential flow, especially when we compare it with the outflow of investment income for the same period. In the years 1971–76, remittances averaged 57.6 percent of net investment income outflow. For the same period, remittances averaged 10 percent of Jamaica's exports.

The relationship between these annual remittances and past emigration is influenced by a number of factors, among them the size of past emigration, the economic condition of the emigrant in his new country, and the number of dependents left behind in his home country. In general, as the emigrant settles down in his new country and brings his family over to join him, the flow of remittances tends to decline sharply.[18]

This brings up the interesting question of the implication of the new U.S. immigration policy which emphasizes the reuniting of families. As more families are reunited, the less need there will be for sending money home. One would therefore not expect remittances from the United States to grow significantly in the future, despite the increased emigration since the latter part of the 1960s.

THE COST OF MIGRATION

Any attempt to measure the cost of migration to the sending country must be at best speculative, for so many factors are involved. If the emigrants were homogeneous, were all trained locally at public expense, were fully employed at the time of their migration, and received similar incomes, we would be able to come up with a pretty fair assessment of the short- and long-run cost of their emigration. Reality, of course, is far more complicated; the emigrants do not possess the ideal characteristics above, except perhaps in small subgroups. Thus the problem of estimating the cost in terms of such measures as: expenditures on education; savings, output, and consumption foregone; productivity per worker, and so on, is fraught with a number of pitfalls. Furthermore, a number of social and political implications must also be considered. Migration may increase the social well-being of a family if only because it thinks that an emigrant family member will improve his situation, thereby making the family generally better off. Social and political tension in the sending country may be relieved if certain politically active groups migrate. Such a reduction of tension could provide the stability and certainty necessary for long-range planning by the private sector as well as the government. On the other hand, a reduction of tension may lead to a relaxation of efforts by the society and its leaders to solve difficult domestic problems; it may also lead to the perpetration of unworkable systems because of the absence of critical appraisal by opposing groups. All of these things would eventually have economic effects but they would be difficult to measure.

R. K. Girling has provided a rough estimate of the cost of skilled migration from Jamaica. As he puts it:

> Using a 7 percent discount rate [the current capital costs] come to J$815 for an average 16 years of education. On this basis, the average undiscounted cost to Jamaica of "producing" each technical and professional emigrant is J$4,481. Thus the total value of the annual "gift" of human capital [based on 1966–68 immigration figures] to the metropolitan nations by Jamaica is almost J$9 million, accounting for only the highly skilled.[19]

Girling qualifies this by indicating that not all the costs are borne by the government; some are financed by private tution charges and limited external subsidies. Many professionals are trained abroad using their own resources or the resources of the institutions at which they are trained. When some of these people ultimately show up in the migration statistics, as they frequently do, allowance must be made in any estimate of human capital outflow, unless it is assumed that the sending country lays claim to human capital regardless of the source of its development.

R. W. Palmer has made some rough estimates of output and consumption foregone as a result of emigration from Jamaica to the United States between 1963 and 1972.[20] He assumed that all the workers who migrated to the United States were employed and had a source of income to satisfy the U.S. embassy visa officers prior to migration. On the basis of this assumption, annual output foregone was calculated by multiplying the per capita output of the classifiable labor force in Jamaica by the number of emigrant workers. In 1972 this came to (J) $10.4 million, which was roughly 8 percent of the increase of the GDP (in purchasers' values at current prices) that year. On the basis of the same formula, output foregone in 1975 was (J) $15 million, or 4 percent of the increment in the GDP. It is hard to verify whether or not these figures reflect the actual reduction in the rate of growth of GDP since so many other factors influence that growth. However, given the significance of skilled workers in the migration flow, it is difficult to expect that flow to have anything but a negative effect on the growth of output in a country where skills are in short supply.

If output is foregone as a result of migration, so is consumption. Again, if the emigrants were homogeneous with the same pattern of consumption, we could make a fair assessment of what kinds of production and imports would be affected by their departure. If, for example, they were all from the upper income group, we would be certain that their departure would reduce the consumption of high value-added items, a substantial share of which would be imported. In fact, the consumption of domestically produced foods may be little affected by their migration. In the absence of this ideal situation, we have to resort to a rough formula which defines personal consumption foregone as per capita personal consumption expenditures of the population times the total number of emigrants. For 1975, this was (J) $9.3 million, or 3 percent of the increase in personal consumption expenditures.

These calculations suggest that migration has had a greater negative impact on incremental output than on incremental consumption. One implication is that inflationary pressure will tend to intensify. It also means that the growth of savings will decline, with obvious consequences for future capital formation and economic growth.

NOTES

1. George W. Roberts, "Prospects for Population Growth in the West Indies," *Social and Economic Studies* 11 (1962): 333–50.

2. Ibid., p. 339.

3. Ibid.

4. George W. Roberts, "Provisional Assessment of Growth of the Kingston-St. Andrew Area, 1960–1970," *Social and Economic Studies* 12 (1963): 435.

5. George C. Abbott, "Estimates of the Growth of the Population of the West Indies to 1975," *Social and Economic Studies* 12 (1963): 242–43.

6. Roberts, "Prospects," op. cit., p. 349.

7. Sonia S. Sinclair, "A Fertility Analysis of Jamaica," *Social and Economic Studies* 23 (1974): 597.

8. See U.S. Department of Labor, *Immigrants and the American Labor Market*, Manpower Research Monograph No. 31 (Washington, D.C.: Government Printing Office, 1974), p. 10.

9. Franklin Abrams, "Immigration Law and Its Enforcement: Reflections of American Immigration," paper presented at a conference sponsored by the Research Institute on Immigration and Ethnic Studies, Smithsonian Institution, Washington, D.C., November 1976, p. 21. (Mimeographed.)

10. Ibid., p. 37.

11. Robert L. Aronson, "Labour Commitment Among Bauxite Workers," *Social and Economic Studies* 10 (1961): 181.

12. Part of this may be explained by the recruitment of workers from St. Lucia and St. Vincent to reap sugar cane during 1968–74. See Erskine Ward, "The Industry Survives," *The Bajan* (1976): 18–20.

13. Trinidad and Tobago, *Third Five Year Plan 1969–1973 (Draft)* (Port-of-Spain: Government Printery, 1969), p. 169.

14. Carl Stone, "Of Jobs and Politics," *Jamaica Weekly Gleaner (NA)*, July 3, 1978, p. 11.

15. Josh DeWind et al., "The Cane Contract: West Indians in Florida," *NACLA Report on the Americas* 11 (1977): 11–17.

16. Ibid., p. 11.

17. Ibid., p. 15.

18. A study by Ian M. Hume of the emigration of southern Europeans to both France and West Germany confirms this pattern. "Migrant Workers in Europe," *Finance and Development* 10 (1973): 2–6.

19. R. K. Girling, "The Migration of Human Capital from the Third World: The Implications and Some Data on the Jamaican Case," *Social and Economic Studies* 23 (1974): 92.

20. R. W. Palmer, "A Decade of West Indian Migration to the United States, 1962–1972: An Economic Analysis," *Social and Economic Studies* 23 (1974): 571–87.

7

Caribbean Development and U.S. Policy

The migration of human resources from the Caribbean to the United States, the growing financial indebtedness of Caribbean countries to the United States, and the dominance of the growth points of the Caribbean economy by U.S. direct investment all underscore the economic—and by implication, the political—role of the United States in the Caribbean. No U.S. policy toward the Caribbean can fail to take into account these facts.

National security objectives have traditionally guided U.S. policy toward the region. While the strategic military importance of the Caribbean to the United States has declined, the economic importance of the region has grown. The United States is the major supplier of foreign capital and food to the Caribbean, and the Caribbean is now a major supplier of labor and raw materials to the United States. It is not unreasonable to suggest that in economic terms, the Caribbean was never more important for the national security of the United States.

Yet in the Caribbean there is widespread poverty. The fact that poverty is so persistent at the doorstep of the richest capitalist nation which has reaped substantial profits from investment in the region suggests that Caribbean development strategy with its overt dependence on foreign direct investment—especially U.S. investment—has not been an unqualified success for the region. From Jamaica to Guyana, governments are experimenting with new strategies in an effort to eliminate what are regarded as the unacceptable features of past industrial development strategies.

The international dimension of the new strategies include new alliances with a wide range of international organizations and new domestic institutions to develop the leverage required to deal with the rich nations in the international marketplace. Of particular importance is the fact that the Caribbean countries have ostensibly identified themselves with Third World countries and have been in the forefront of the drive for a new international economic order.

THE NEW INTERNATIONAL ECONOMIC ORDER

Developing countries perceive the international market mechanism as operating in favor of the advanced countries whose disproportionate market power influences the outcome of prices. The exchange relationship which is the essence of the market mechanism is a power relationship, and the developing countries—especially the non-oil-producing ones—feel that the existing rules of the game offer little prospect for achieving what they regard as a more equitable distribution of the gains from world trade. Because many developing countries depend heavily on the export of raw materials to the advanced countries, and because the prices of these commodities have historically been unstable, the focus of the call for a new international economic order has been on stability in commodity markets.

The principal technique for achieving stability in commodity markets in the United Nations Conference on Trade and Development (UNCTAD) Integrated Program is the concept of "buffer stocks." The idea is that if enough financing is available to create a Common Fund to finance buffer stocks of the ten core commodities which account for the major share of the value of the commodity exports of the developing countries, prices would be stabilized at a high level. The United States has officially opposed the Common Fund. According to the *International Economic Report of the President*,

> the United States opposes the Common Fund, which, it believes, is based on a number of fundamental misconceptions including: (1) the expectation that higher commodity prices will result from a Common Fund and will primarily benefit the developing countries, and (2) the belief that lack of financing has been the major roadblock in creating buffer stocks. In the U.S. view, the use of a Common Fund to achieve higher prices artificially would be of greater benefit to the developed countries—Australia, Canada, South Africa, and the United States—which account for about 70 percent of world commodity exports and a similar share of storable commodities. Secondly, the obstacle to buffer stocks has been not the lack of financing but rather lack of agreement by exporters and importers on the price to be supported and the uncertain feasibility of buffer stocks for many commodities.[1]

U.S. opposition to commodity price stabilization arrangements is also articulated by a number of American academicians. Nathaniel Leff of Columbia University argues that since most Third World countries import as well as export primary products, the effects of higher commodity prices on individual countries

> will depend on the price increases in specific commodities and on the composition of each country's exports and imports. Taking account of the

effects of increased import prices on developing countries, the net impact of a high overall level of commodity prices on many Third World countries is likely to be far less favourable than they expected. [2]

Sjaastad of the University of Chicago takes the following view:

The basic issue concerning any commodity market intervention scheme is what is to be stabilized and at what level. Most discussions, at least at the popular level, focus on price stabilization, but implicit in the supporting arguments is the unstated assumption that price stability will also result in stability of export earnings (and hence import costs). That is, of course, sheer nonsense for most agricultural commodities where the main source of instability is in production itself. As any farmer knows, shifts in supply cause price and quantity to move in opposite directions so that the income of those producers responsible for the supply shifts is much less affected than is the price itself. As nine of the twelve main commodity exports of Latin America are of agricultural origin, it makes little sense to talk about price stabilization as a means of reducing the instability in the foreign exchange earnings from those sources. Indeed, if a way were found to stabilize those prices, the variability in export earnings would be increased rather than reduced, as a fall in production would not be matched with an increase in the world price. The real benefits of such a scheme would accrue to the consumers, not the producers. [3]

Sjaastad makes several other points:

that price stabilization schemes are intended to raise prices, not to stabilize them;
that what is proposed is really an international cartel in disguise;
that such a scheme would generate an uncontrolled accumulation of surplus production;
that commodity price supports are typically not enjoyed by the producers but rather by the governments of the exporting countries which control marketing monopolies. Consequently, price-elevating commodity agreements would subject U.S. consumers to indirect taxation by foreign governments;
that artificially high prices would attract inefficient producers whose vested interest in high price becomes converted into political pressure to avoid price reductions; and
that international cooperation is not an essential ingredient for price stabilization since this can be accomplished by individual countries with an export duty when prices are high and a subsidy when they are low. [4]

These objections to integrated commodity programs miss the essential point insofar as they insist on the unrestrained operation of the market mechanism to provide an acceptable equilibrium solution. The essential problem which the international economic order seeks to address is that of distribution. The market mechanism has been notorious for its inability to solve this problem, largely because distribution is also a social and political objective, and also because there is little unanimity on what constitutes equitable distribution of the world's resources. It is generally agreed, however, that some redistribution must occur. According to the Report by the Secretary General of the United Nations Conference on Trade and Development to UNCTAD IV:

> It is inconceivable that the developed countries can continue on a smooth and even course of growth and rising prosperity within a global framework in which the vast mass of people, inhabiting the greater part of the planet, continues to remain in a state of unrest. This, in the last analysis, is the stake of the developed countries in the successful resolution of the development problem. Their response to third world demands cannot be based on a narrow reckoning of immediate costs and benefits, or resources gained and foregone. It needs to be set in the wider perspective of the evolving pattern of global relationships—political as well as social. [5]

Thus a wider concept of development is necessary to assure global order. Angelos Angelopolous' thoughts on development are particularly relevant here:

> A larger, more equitable, and more human conception should be given to the idea of development. The objective of development consists not only of the accumulation of goods but also and primarily of the promotion of the interests of the human being as an integral whole. Development is thus a process of structural change in economic, social, political, and cultural domains. Development must be carried out for the benefit of all and not of a small minority. It is a collective effort and its fruits must be equitably distributed among all who participate. [6]

ECONOMIC COOPERATION IN THE CARIBBEAN

The new international economic order can provide only a general framework within which specific policies for Caribbean development must be formulated. Over and above the general question of a redistribution of the gains from world trade is the question of the collective viability of the small Caribbean economies. The long historical and cultural relationship between the Caribbean and the United States mandates a serious U.S. commitment toward the development of the region.

The U.S. posture toward the Caribbean in recent years has exhibited a preference for a regional approach to development as evidenced by a statement by the U.S. assistant secretary for InterAmerican Affairs:

> We are committed to support strengthened cooperation among the Caribbean states themselves. In the Caribbean, the whole is more than the sum of its parts. So long as its peoples remain isolated from each other, instability and

dependence on others are likely to persist. The resources of the area will be used inefficiently, and political and social energies will be dissipated.[7]

The implication here is that an integrated Caribbean is the best path toward solving the region's economic problems. There is undoubtedly a great deal of merit to this approach: wider domestic markets, greater specialization, and so forth. This view is similar to the one so eloquently expressed by William Demas, the Governor of the Caribbean Development Bank:

> It is the apparently congenital tendency of the English-speaking Caribbean countries toward fragmentation and the resultant external dependence. We all know, however, that what appears to be a genetic characteristic is the product of powerful historical factors which from the very beginning of the European penetration some three hundred years ago produced competitive and not complementary approaches to development as between the "West India Colonies." This early history of economic fragmentation produces stronger links between each West Indian Colony and the European metropolis than obtained between the neighbouring colonies themselves and, because of metropolitan "exclusivity," led to often fierce competition on the part of each colony to gain short-run economic advantage at the expense of others. Individual country external economic dependence on the metropolis precluded greater economic interdependence between the West Indian countries.
>
> To use the language of the mathematicians, development was conceived of in each territory as a "zero sum game"—that is, one in which one could only gain at the expense of one's neighbour. The idea of economic co-operation and economic integration as leading to a situation in which all could mutually gain is therefore one which not surprisingly is long in taking firm roots in our part of the world. Yet what can be simpler than the proposition that the development of neighbouring countries—each with a small national market, an insufficient range of human resources and a narrow range of natural resources considered individually, but collectively endowed with a much bigger market, a reasonably balanced pool of human skills and a fairly good natural resource base in relation to their population—can only be meaningfully promoted within a framework of close collaboration and co-ordination rather than one of individual effort combined with wasteful and unhealthy competition and very expensive duplication of economic activities and infrastructural facilities? And in using the term "development" here, I refer not only to production and infrastructure but also to other areas where co-ordination, joint actions and common policies are beneficial to all—areas such as Sea and Air Transportation; University Education; Foreign Investment and the Adaption and Transfer of Technology; and above all, External Trade and other Economic Relations, including obviously desirable relations of closer economic co-operation with other Caribbean and Latin American countries as well as with other countries and groups of countries in the world.[8]

Advocacy by the United States of regional cooperation is in an important way predicated upon a vigorous role for the private sector. In other words, the development of the Caribbean is seen as occurring through regional cooperation with the private sector playing a pivotal role. As Todman puts it:

> The volume of investment required and the need for functional, long-term relationships and institutions in the development process both point to the indispensable role of private sector activity.
>
> The individual decisions of American businessmen and companies to become involved in industry or tourism in one of the Caribbean nations, to engage in import or export trade, to open a plant, to invest in local enterprise, to arrange financing, to cooperate with a Caribbean government or company in a joint venture—these are the kinds of activities which, as a whole, will affect the economic future of the Caribbean far more than the official transactions of the U.S. Government.
>
> They will also affect the climate of U.S.-Caribbean relations itself.[9]

Yet the kind of institutional setting required to make economic integration in the Caribbean work may not necessarily be accommodating to the individual decisions of American businessmen. Andrew Axline argues that "since effective regional integration for development requires a 'dirigiste' integration programme to effect political control over trade and investment, and to implement economic planning on a region-wide basis success will depend on the move toward more 'socialist' oriented types of political regimes."[10]

A number of factors militate against the process toward economic integration in the region, not the least among them are the recent proliferation of bilateral arrangements with countries outside CARICOM, the rash of new international producer organizations, and the new trade concessions won from the EEC under the Lomé Convention. Axline views the provisions of the Lomé Convention which require investment from EEC countries to be treated in equal status with that of nationals of ACP countries as "a further impediment to the adoption of an effective regional policy on foreign investment."[11] Hans-Joerg Geiser, however, contends that "despite the selective and divisive aspects of the new Lomé regime there are certain positive provisions in the Convention which will serve as a bridge between the independent and nonindependent CARICOM members and which, in the long run, will also have an integrating effect on CARICOM as a whole."[12]

The serious balance-of-payments difficulties of Jamaica and Guyana in the 1970s have shaken the weak foundations of CARICOM as national governments pursue trade-restricting strategies in search of equilibrium. Yet there are some vital signs that are encouraging. A regional food plan is being developed; initial steps have been taken to establish a common external tariff; a temporary facility for assisting countries with their balance-of-payments difficulties has been created; and action on the harmonization of fiscal incentives has begun.

THE CARIBBEAN DEVELOPMENT FACILITY

While foreign private investment in the Caribbean will continue to be important in the years ahead, there will probably have to be an increased flow through nontraditional channels such as regional organizations like the Caribbean Development Bank (CDB) for its reallocation into investment ventures throughout the Caribbean to enhance indigenous sources of development.

There appear to be the beginnings of an enlightened U.S. policy toward this end. A big step forward is the recognition that U.S. policy must complement rather than compete with Caribbean policy to encourage economic progress in the region. In this direction, the United States has made an important symbolic move by joining with some 25 Caribbean and non-Caribbean countries to establish the Caribbean Group for Cooperation in Economic Development. According to the World Bank, the Caribbean Group is to serve as a "mechanism for the coordination and strengthening of external assistance to the Caribbean and for the continuing review of national and regional activities related to economic development of the area."[13]

At its first meeting in June 1978, the Caribbean Group agreed to establish the Caribbean Development Facility (CDF) "as a mechanism for channeling foreign resources to help finance essential imports and to offer supplementary financing—mainly for local costs—to assist in the execution of development programs and projects."[14] The CDF is viewed as a temporary facility for allowing hard-pressed Caribbean governments to maintain "acceptable levels of development" while pursuing (for a period of no more than five years) austerity programs designed to achieve financial stability. In the present Caribbean context, this is essentially a rescue operation to save ongoing projects which have been threatened by severe balance-of-payments difficulties, and, in the case of Jamaica, by the harsh conditions imposed by the IMF in return for providing balance-of-payments relief.

The Caribbean Group will act as broker to obtain financing from multiple donors for distribution to multiple recipients. A working group made up of the International Bank for Reconstruction and Development (IBRD), the IMF, the Inter-American Development Bank, and the CDB will estimate the amount of CDF financing required each year and make recommendations on the eligibility of individual recipient countries based upon the existence of appropriate short- and medium-term economic policies. The initial amount of funds pledged to the CDF by ten donor countries in June 1978 was $112 million; the United States has pledged to meet 30 percent of this amount. The need for financing of the CDF type is expected to average $125 million annually. The World Bank estimates that external official capital assistance required by the Caribbean over the years 1979–81 will average $650 million per year, two-thirds of which will be made available on Official Development Assistance (ODA) forms.[15] Contributions to the CDF by donor countries will not in any way affect ongoing bilateral arrangements with recipient countries.

The Caribbean Group will broaden the range of contact of the Caribbean governments both within and without the Caribbean. It will provide a mechanism through which a wide range of important organizations* which are associated may provide financial assistance to the Caribbean.

Because the Caribbean countries are ministates with individual economic problems that cannot adequately be dealt with by traditional international institutions, the Caribbean Group is regarded as the prototype of a new structure for handling the peculiar problems of ministates all over the world. The principle, of course, is not new. In 1976 the government of Trinidad and Tobago, in cooperation with Jamaica, Guyana, and Barbados, established the Balance of Payments Mutual Support Interim Facility to provide financial assistance to members with balance-of-payments difficulties.†

The CDF is essentially a larger version of the Interim Facility. It is expected to have a positive impact on CARICOM trade by stimulating the removal of important restrictions imposed over the last few years by member countries with serious balance of payments problems.

TOWARD A U.S. POLICY FOR REGIONAL CARIBBEAN DEVELOPMENT

The primary objective of U.S. policy should be to encourage the development of existing and new regional channels through which resources can flow to the Caribbean to develop a strong indigenous economic foundation. These channels must operate on two levels: the government and the private. At the government level, the Caribbean Development Bank is one pivotal regional institution through which U.S. development funding should be channeled. At the private level, the U.S. multinational corporation in the Caribbean represents an important channel through which an enlightened U.S. development policy for indigenous regional development may be effected. U.S. tax measures should be explicitly designed to encourage these multinationals to make a greater contribution toward local development by inducing them to invest a larger share of their profits into local development-oriented projects. This means that the

---

*These organizations include international bodies such as OPEC, IDB, the International Fund for Agricultural Development (IFAD), and the United Nations Development Programme (UNDP).

†The objectives of CDF are: to promote the development of intraregional trade; to supplement other sources of balance-of-payments support with an immediately available additional source of funds; and to help sustain the capacity of the members to finance imports necessary to help their development objectives.

United States must actively support the harmonization of fiscal incentives in the region in order to avoid numerous bilateral arrangements.

Because the U.S. demand for the major Caribbean export goods typically takes the form of intraindustry transactions, U.S. policy should support the establishment of a regional organization to monitor the transfer-pricing behavior of the multinational firms to ensure that such behavior is not inimical to the best economic interests of the host country.

There are serious distributional problems in the Caribbean which can be effectively solved only if the distributional problem in the larger international arena is solved. The United States has steadfastly opposed UNCTAD proposals for an integrated commodity agreement, largely because of its fear of international cartels. Because Caribbean governments identify themselves closely with Third World economic aspirations, and in fact are leading advocates of Third World proposals for a new international economic order, U.S. policy toward the Caribbean must attempt to address the concerns that are embodied in these proposals.

NOTES

1. *International Economic Report of the President.* (Washington, D.C.: Government Printing Office, 1977).

2. Nathaniel H. Leff, "The New Economic Order—Bad Economics, Worse Politics," *Foreign Policy* (1976): 204.

3. *U.S. Economic Relations with Latin America*, Hearings before the Subcommittee on Inter-American Economic Relationships of the Joint Economic Committee, Congress of the United States, 94th Cong., 2d sess. (Washington, D.C.: Government Printing Office, 1977), pp. 298–99.

4. Ibid., pp. 298–301.

5. *New Directions and New Structures for Trade and Development*, Report by the Secretary-General of the United Nations Conference on Trade and Development to UNCTAD IV, TD/183/Rev. 1 (New York: United Nations, 1977), p. 2.

6. Angelos Th. Angelopolous, *For a New Policy of International Development* (New York: Praeger Publishers, 1977), p. 81.

7. Keynote address by Terence A. Todman, U.S. Assistant Secretary of State for InterAmerican Affairs, at the 2nd Caribbean Conference on Trade, Investment and Development, January 18, 1978, Miami (mimeographed), p. 8.

8. William G. Demas, "CDB: A Bank and a Development Instrument," statement by the President of the Caribbean Development Bank at the Seventh Annual Meeting of the Board of Governors in Port-of-Spain, April 1977.

9. Todman, op. cit., p. 10.

10. W. Andrew Axline, "Autonomy and Integration: The Issue of Caribbean International Relations," paper presented at the Seminar on Political and Economic Choices in the Contemporary Caribbean, Woodrow Wilson International Center for Scholars, Smithsonian Institution, Washington, D.C., February 1978, p. 5.

11. Ibid., p. 4.

12. Hans-Joerg Geiser, "The Lomé Convention and Caribbean Integration: A First Assessment," *Revista Review InterAmericana* 6 (1976): 46.

13. World Bank News Release, June 26, 1978, p. 1.

14. Ibid.

15. Ibid., p. 2.

Appendix A

Getting Control of a Commanding Height: The Jamaican Bauxite Industry

THE BAUXITE PRODUCTION LEVY

In its attempt to counter the adverse effects of the abrupt increase in petroleum prices in 1973 and the worldwide recession-cum-inflation which ensued, the Jamaican government took steps to increase its revenues from its most important export industry—the bauxite industry. In 1974 the government requested a 700 percent increase in bauxite revenues from the industry, which is owned largely by U.S. multinational firms. After long and sometimes heated negotiations failed to reach a mutual agreement, the government legislated such an increase in the form of the Bauxite Production Levy Act. This act set a minimum production level of 14 million long dry tons (LDT) (or about 90 percent of total production capacity) for the industry and tied the tax revenues from bauxite to the average realized price (ARP) of primary aluminum in the United States over a calendar year. It also established the Capital Development Fund to receive the proceeds of the production levy.

Table A.1 shows the dramatic increase in government revenues in 1974 resulting from the production levy, which is imposed on one LDT of bauxite at the rate of 7.5 percent of the ARP of one short ton of primary aluminum.[1] In the aftermath of this production levy, if a 1 percent change in the value of U.S. aluminum production were due exclusively to a change in the price per ton of primary aluminum, the impact on government revenues from the bauxite industry would be substantial. According to the Jamaica Bauxite Institute (JBI),

> at a levy rate of $7\frac{1}{2}$ percent, each one cent movement in the ARP gives an increase or decrease of 35 cents in the production levy rate per ton of bauxite. This movement in the ARP is even more significant when we think of it in terms of a total annual minimum of 13 million LDT, each one cent move would result in a difference of U.S. $4.55 million.[2]

Two features of the bauxite levy are innovative: the minimum level of production and the base of the production tax. According to Malcolm Gillis and Charles McLure, the minimum level of production requirement

> prevent[s] the majors from holding Jamaica hostage by temporarily shifting production to their mines in other countries and thereby depressing the Jamaican economy. To the contrary, Jamaica in effect is holding the firms hostage. As a tax must be paid whether the bauxite is mined or not, the only economical thing to do is to mine at least the minimum amount.[3]

Gillis and McLure argue that most of the production tax is likely to be exported in the short run with the long-run situation depending on the extent to which the International Bauxite Association (IBA) members act in concert.[4] If producers are able to shift the tax forward in the form of higher prices for aluminum ingot, the increases are likely to be slight. Because the production levy

TABLE A.1

Government Revenue from the Bauxite/Alumina Industry, 1972–75
(J $ million)

Year	Royalties	Corporate Taxes	Production Levy (net of corporate tax)	Total
1972	3.07	19.64	0.0	22.71
1973	3.44	21.07	0.0	24.51
1974	7.17	20.27	142.80	170.34
1975	5.40	14.90	121.1	141.4

Source: Jamaica Bauxite Institute.

is indexed to the price of primary aluminum, Jamaica also stands to gain from any forward shifting. Arthur Wright poses the problem this way:

> Assume for simplicity that foreigners now own all the rights to Jamaican bauxite, and that Jamaicans now consume a negligible proportion of world output of aluminum products. Then, without a cartel, Jamaica can tax away (or otherwise secure) production rents at the expense of the current foreign owners. With a cartel, however, Jamaica will be able to reap in addition a transfer of wealth from foreign consumers of aluminum products and also to foist upon the non-bauxite-producing world some amount of deadweight loss. [5]

The Jamaica bauxite levy, tied to the price of ingot and requiring a minimum production level, must rank as one of the finer strategies by a developing country to increase its share of the gains from commercial exploitation of its natural resources while at the same time insulating its revenues against inflation abroad. The danger lies in the long run where advancing technology may be able to reduce the cost of extracting alumina from potential bauxite substitutes such as dawsonite or oil shale, which is plentiful in the United States; and to reduce the transportation cost. It is also conceivable that a shift in the U.S. tax structure favoring the importation of aluminum would encourage U.S. firms to build reduction plants in bauxite-producing countries with the potential for generating vast quantities of cheap electricity (which Jamaica does not have).

THE DEMAND FOR BAUXITE AND ALUMINA

In its 1974 special report on critical imported materials, the U.S. Council on International Economic Policy stated that "U.S. companies currently obtain Jamaican bauxite at a cost of about $15 per ton, including taxes and royalty payments in the range of $2–$3 per ton." [6] The report claims that a doubling of bauxite cost to $30 per ton would add less than 10 percent to the price of aluminum—an increase which would lead to "only limited substitution of aluminum in some uses with steel, plastic, and copper. It would also have little effect on U.S. bauxite production. If the cost exceeds $30 per ton, other aluminum bearing ore such as clays, anorthosite, alunite, and dawsonite may become competitive with bauxite." [7]

One study shows that the U.S. demand for aluminum is relatively insensitive to price changes. It estimates that "a 10 percent increase in the price of aluminum would result in a 2.1 percent short-run reduction in quantity demanded and a 3.8 percent reduction in the long run." [8] For the world as a whole, demand is even more insensitive to prices; the short- and long-run elasticities are estimated to be 0.11 and 0.23, respectively. [9] The study estimates that in the United States, copper is more readily substitutable for aluminum than is aluminum for copper: "In the short run, a 10 percent increase in the price of copper would result in a 0.3 percent short run increase in the demand for aluminum, whereas a 10 percent increase in the price of aluminum would result in an increase in the short run demand for copper of 1.5 percent." [10] Table A.2 shows the industrial production (income) elasticities of demand for aluminum for the United States, Europe, and the total world. Income elasticities for the United States and the total world are slightly higher than those for Europe. For the United States and the world, a 10 percent change in income (production) in the short run would bring about a 7 percent change in the quantity of aluminum demanded. This inelasticity is attributed to the highly capital-intensive nature of

TABLE A.2

Income Elasticities of Demand for Aluminum for Selected Areas

Region	Short Run	Long Run
United States	0.69	1.26
Europe	0.43	1.03
Total world	0.69	1.00

Source: Synergy, Inc., *Joint Aluminum/Copper Forecasting and Simulation Model*, 1977.

the industry. In the long run, the demand for aluminum is generally relatively income elastic with the U.S. demand showing the greatest income elasticity. Price is not the only factor affecting the substitution of one raw material for another. As William Vogley puts it:

> The producer is seeking the lowest cost for the total production function for the product concerned. Since raw materials are usually a relatively small portion of the total cost of the final product, non-cost attributes of the raw material and its indirect effect on other costs may well outweigh any price differentials between the competing inputs. . . . The essential point here is that substitutions between materials may arise from developments completely outside of the price behavior of materials.[11]

Norman Girvan calculates that the ratio of the gross value of one short ton of aluminum to the amount of bauxite required to produce it is 15:1.[12] This means that if the cost of all other factors remains constant, a doubling of the cost of the bauxite input would increase the value of one short ton of aluminum by 6.7 percent. Earlier we indicated that the demand for aluminum is price inelastic. Since demand for bauxite is derived from the demand for aluminum and since the cost of bauxite inputs is a small share of the total cost of aluminum production, it follows that the demand for bauxite must also be price inelastic.

JOINT OWNERSHIP OF THE INDUSTRY

In addition to increasing revenues, the Jamaican government was anxious to recover bauxite lands and to share in the equity of the industry. In October 1976 it signed an agreement with the Aluminum Company of America (Alcoa), which has the largest bauxite mining and processing operations in Jamaica. To quote Prime Minister Manley:

> this agreement embodies the acceptance by Alcoa, the world's leading aluminum producer, of the principle of national control of Jamaica's bauxite resources. At the same time it provides Alcoa with a guaranteed long-term ore supply and predictability of a major cost factor, thereby establishing a secure and stable business environment in which to operate. . . .
> National control embodies four essential requirements:
> [1] That the mining lands acquired by the companies should revert to national ownership;
> [2] That the government should have a majority interest in all mining activity;
> [3] That the government should have the option to participate in any processing operation;
> [4] And, that the government should get a fair return for the exploitation of the country's major physical resource; that is, as primary producers, our return should reflect a consequential relationship to the real value of aluminum ingot in the marketplace. . . .

The major points of the agreement are as follows:

[1] The government will acquire all mining and non-operating lands held by Alcoa Minerals of Jamaica, at a cost not exceeding the original acquisition cost. Some 7,000 acres are involved at a cost of roughly $2.5 million. Promissory notes will be issued for individual parcels contained in current mining plans. For the rest, the government will pay 10 per cent down, the remainder in nine annual installments at 7 per cent interest;

[2] The government will purchase a 51 per cent interest in the mining assets which includes equipment, facilities, land and infra-structure support of the mining as distinct from the alumina processing operation. The replacement value of the assets being acquired is $18 million. However, our share will be acquired at book value which means we are purchasing some $18 million of replaceable assets for approximately $8 million. The method of payment will be 10 per cent down, and in remainder in nine annual installments at 8.5 per cent interest. However, under a formula proposed by the government this 51 per cent share of the mining operation has been converted into a proportionate shareholding of the total mining, processing and shipping facilities of Alcoa Jamaica. This includes the 550,000 tons alumina processing plant at Halse Hall, Clarendon, which has now an estimated replacement value of $300 million. Under this arrangement we will be entitled to receive up to 33 thousand tons of alumina per year which we may, if we choose, market ourselves;

[3] The general agreement covers a period of 40 years from January 1, 1976. This involves a special mining lease which will make ore reserves available to the company for 40 years based on the present capacity of the plant. However, provision is made for expansion.[13]

The book value of Jamaica's 51 percent share of Alcoa's mining operations was (J) $8 million. This was converted into a 6 percent share of the combined mining and processing operations, meaning that the total book value of Alcoa's mining and processing operations in Jamaica in 1976 was (J) $133 million. (The U.S. dollar equivalent at 1976 exchange rates was $147 million.) This represented 25 percent of all U.S. direct investment in Jamaica and 49 percent of U.S. direct investment in mining.

In February 1977 the Jamaica government signed an agreement with the Kaiser Bauxite Company. Kaiser, unlike other U.S. aluminum firms, is totally dependent on Jamaica for bauxite. The agreement provided that Kaiser: sell to the government its 50,000 acres of bauxite lands at book value; lease back those lands from the government for 40 years; sell to the government 51 percent ownership of its bauxite operations at a book value of $5.61 million. Kaiser will manage the company for the first seven years of the partnership with its board of directors shared equally with the government. The agreement provided Kaiser with a secure and steady source of bauxite, a point the company regards as paramount. The agreement also guarantees the government a rate of return of 14.68 percent on its investment.

The Jamaica government reached a similar agreement with the Reynolds Bauxite Company. The government will purchase a 51 percent majority ownership with control of the executive committee. It will get back 65,000 acres of bauxite lands, including agricultural and cold storage operations. Lands required to carry out mining operations will be allocated to the company. Reserve lands will be utilized by the government for agricultural and other purposes until they are required for mining. The size of each allocation of reserve lands to the bauxite company is determined by the area required to support bauxite production over a five- to seven-year period.

National control is seen as facilitating "the most orderly and productive use of ore reserve lands before, during and after mining. Before mining, the land is available for leasing or government farms. After mining and restoration it becomes available for permanent crops or settlement. Where the companies had themselves farmed, leased to or settled small holders, these programs will be maintained."[14] Negotiations are currently underway with the Aluminum Company of Canada (Alcan) and the Aluminum Partners of Jamaica (Alpart), which is owned by Kaiser, Reynolds, and Anaconda.

THE DEVELOPMENT OF LINKAGES

The localization of ownership is the first stage in the strategy to develop incremental capacity in a manner which creates greater value-added locally. The centerpiece of the second stage is the construction of smelter capacity. Such a smelter would become the hub around which a variety of industrial linkages could develop, and it is here that regional collaboration is of the utmost importance because of the large capital and energy requirements.

Since Jamaica has no abundant source of cheap electric power, the suggestion has been made that the power requirements for a 400,000-ton capacity smelter could be provided by a nuclear power plant with a capacity of 1,000 megawatts.[15] The problem that Jamaica faces is that it is more economical to locate smelters at the source of cheap energy. In the United States, for example, 30 percent of the primary aluminum capacity is located in the Pacific Northwest, where the cheapest power is available from the federal government's Bonneville Power Administration, the major power supplier in that area.

But even where power is abundant and cheap, the aluminum industry is faced with

> significantly increasing costs. . . . The Bonneville Power Administration . . .
> announced in 1976 that drastic modifications and curtailments would apply to
> the aluminum power contracts upon their expiration in the mid 1980's. . . . A
> plan proposed by the Pacific Northwest Utilities Conference Committee,
> which would go into effect immediately, subject to Congressional ratification,
> would ensure the aluminum companies a long-term source of power, but at

significantly higher rates. The plan would authorize power from selected non-federal generating facilities, including thermal systems.[16]

Over the last few years, Jamaica has participated in joint proposals with other Caribbean countries to construct aluminum smelters. In all cases, the proposed smelters would be located close to the energy source—in Trinidad and Tobago, Guyana, or Mexico. In 1975 the first two regional aluminum smelters proposed by Jamaica, Trinidad, and Guyana were to be constructed in Trinidad and Tobago and Guyana. The estimated cost of the Trinidad smelter with an annual capacity of 75,000 tons was $150 million. The proposed Guyana smelter had a capacity of 150,000 tons a year and would cost $300 million. The plant in Trinidad would get its power from locally produced natural gas, while the Guyana installation would use the hydroelectric power now being harnessed in that country. In Guyana the priority given the proposed smelter was expressed by the minister of finance in his budget speech for 1976: "In order to achieve major forward linkages in the bauxite industry, the Government has been pushing the development of its hydropower resources as a necessary concommitant to the establishment of an aluminium smelter in Guyana."[17] Trinidad Prime Minister Eric Williams, however, did not give the smelter the necessary top priority in his 1976 budget speech, favoring instead those projects ostensibly linked to the petroleum industry.

Regional collaboration on the two smelters, however, has been undermined by the inability of Jamaica and Guyana to contribute their share of the equity, due to their balance-of-payments difficulties, and this situation has prompted Trinidad to go it alone. Presumably, that country will get its aluminum from Surinam and Guyana, if and when its smelter is built.

After the failure of these joint efforts, Jamaica entered a joint venture with Venezuela and Mexico to construct the JAVEMEX alumina project in Jamaica. Jamaica was to have 51 percent ownership; Mexico, up to 29 percent; and Venezuela, up to 10 percent. The principal consumer of alumina from the JAVEMEX project was to be a joint Jamaica-Mexico smelter called JALUMEX to be built in Mexico. Agreements signed between the two governments in 1977 provided for 71 percent Mexican ownership and 29 percent Jamaican ownership. But in May 1978 Mexico withdrew from JALUMEX and indirectly undermined the JAVEMEX alumina project. The Jamaican government announcement of the Mexican withdrawal read in part:

The reasons cited by the Mexican Government for its decision not to proceed with the project is the lower return on investment than when the project was originally conceived, arising largely from the devaluation of the Mexican peso and the increase in costs over the period since it was first put forward. These costs include energy, machinery and equipment and technology.[18]

In view of the failure of regional collaboration in the bauxite and alumina industry, the future integration of the bauxite industry into the Jamaican economy is in serious doubt. A number of new developments in the United States may well militate against the development of smelting capacity in Jamaica. One is the growth of aluminum production from new and old aluminum scrap. Over the past several years, this has accounted for at least 20 percent of the total aluminum supply. In 1976, secondary recovery was 2.9 billion pounds, representing 23 percent of the total supply of aluminum. It is believed that

> the rapidly increasing interest in recycling and municipal solid waste processing will contribute to future growth. . . . Aside from the environmental and financial incentives, the reclamation program is of paramount importance, both for the conservation of primary aluminum and for energy savings. Smelting of secondary aluminum requires only 5 percent of the energy required to produce primary aluminum.[19]

Another development is a joint program by the U.S. Energy Research and Development Administration and a U.S. primary aluminum producer to develop an aluminum smelting process that uses coal instead of electricity for energy.

> The agreement provides for the construction of a small scale pilot plant to explore the feasibility of the process which has been proven only in laboratory operations. An important aspect of the process is that it can use a high proportion of lower grade aluminum ores that are plentiful in the United States.[20]

It would appear that the path to the development of linkages to the bauxite/alumina industry in Jamaica does not lie in the production of aluminum from alumina, since this energy-intensive process is too costly for the island. Rather the path may very well lie in the production of secondary aluminum from aluminum scrap—both locally generated and imported. The energy cost of producing secondary aluminum is estimated to be 5 percent of the cost of producing primary aluminum. Secondary aluminum is used mostly in castings, and castings are used extensively in automobiles. It is "estimated that over 50 percent of the 100 pounds of aluminum being used in the average 1977 [automobile] model consisted of castings. The projected increased automotive use of aluminum, because of its ability to reduce the weight and improve fuel economy, will contribute to the growth of the castings field."[21] Jamaica's potential for becoming a major supplier of a wide range of castings in the Caribbean should be seriously explored.

NOTES

1. According to the Jamaica Bauxite Institute *Annual Report 1976* p. 20:

Average realised price for the levy is the arithmetic average of the weighted average prices per pound of primary aluminum realised by the three U.S. companies, namely Kaiser, Reynolds and Alcoa as determined from their annual Form 10–K Report filed with the U.S. Securities and Exchange Commission.

The rate of levy on one LDT of bauxite is 7.5 percent of the ARP of one short ton (ST) of primary aluminum (including all grades between 99.5 percent and 99.99 percent) divided by 4.3. It is calculated as follows:

$$\frac{7.5 \times \text{ARP per lb.} \times 2,000}{100 \times 4.3}$$

The 4.3 in the denominator is the bauxite equivalent in long dry tons of one short ton (2,000 pounds) of metal. This is based on a bauxite/alumina conversion factor of 2.2 LDT/ST and an alumina/aluminum factor of about 1.95.

The 7.5 percent rate was to be increased by half a percentage point each year to 8.5 percent in 1976, but as an incentive, the government has allowed it to be fixed at 7.5 percent for a number of years for companies which have signed agreements to enter into partnership with the government of Jamaica. Jamaica Bauxite Institute, *Royalties, Income Taxes and the Bauxite Levy 1950–1976* (mimeo, no date).

2. Ibid.

3. Malcolm Gillis and Charles E. McLure, "Incidence of World Taxes on Natural Resources with Special Reference to Bauxite," *American Economic Review* 65 (1975): 395.

4. Ibid.

5. Arthur W. Wright, "Discussion [of papers on the taxation of natural resources]," *American Economic Review* 65 (1975): 406.

6. Council on International Economic Policy, *Special Report: Critical Imported Materials* (Washington, D.C.: Government Printing Office, 1974), p. 28.

7. Ibid.

8. *Joint Aluminum/Copper Forecasting and Simulation Model*, report prepared for the U.S. Department of the Interior, Bureau of Mines, by Synergy, Inc., 1977, p. 84.

9. Ibid.

10. Ibid., p. 85.

11. William A. Vogley, "Resource Substitution," in *U.S. Economic Growth from 1976 to 1986: Prospects, Problems, and Patterns—Resources and Energy* Vol. 4, Joint Economic Committee of the Congress of the United States (Washington, D.C.: Government Printing Office, 1977), pp. 88–89.

12. Norman Girvan, *The Caribbean Bauxite Industry* (Kingston: Institute for Social and Economic Research, University of the West Indies, 1967), p. 3.

13. *JBI Digest* 1 (1976): 3–7.

14. Jamaica Bauxite Institute, *Jamaica and the Bauxite Companies: What the Agreements Mean* (mimeo, no date), p. 4.

15. Girvan, op. cit., p. 23.

16. U.S. Department of Commerce, *U.S. Industrial Outlook 1978* (Washington, D.C.: Government Printing Office, 1977), p. 67.

17. Guyana, *Budget 1976* (Georgetown: Guyana Printers, 1975), p. 27.

18. *Jamaica Weekly Gleaner (NA)*, May 15, 1978, p. 67.

19. *U.S. Industrial Outlook 1978*, op. cit., p. 67. In addition to the 95 percent saving in energy cost

for processing bauxite up through the primary aluminum stage, an OECD study lists the following savings in materials in the production of one ton of recovered (secondary) aluminum:

four tons or more of the basic ore (bauxite), depending upon the quality of the ore;
the materials used to refine the four tons of bauxite into two tons of alumina: 1,000 pounds of soda and 250 pounds of lime;
the materials used to process the two tons of alumina into one ton of primary aluminum: 1,500 pounds of petroleum coke and pitch, 60 pounds of cryolite, and 80 pounds of aluminum flouride.

Organisation for Economic Co-operation and Development, *Industrial Adaptation in the Primary Aluminium Industry* (Paris: OECD, 1976).

20. *U.S. Industrial Outlook 1978*, op. cit., p. 68.

21. Ibid., p. 67.

Appendix B
United States Consumption of Caribbean Tourism

The purpose of this appendix is to explore the implications of the relationship between the consumption of tourist services in Jamaica and Barbados and the disposable income of the consumer, typically the American tourist. Since tourist services are generally considered to be a luxury, we would expect their consumption to be income elastic. We will attempt to measure the extent of this income elasticity and use this measure as a rough basis for making a ten-year projection of a possible expansion path for the industry in Jamaica and Barbados.

A number of obvious factors influence the level of tourist business in those countries: economic conditions in the United States; cost of air transportation; and political conditions in the Caribbean. What is not obvious, however, is the precise extent to which these factors influence the industry. No long-range planning for the industry can afford to ignore the empirical relationship between the demand for tourist services in the Caribbean and changing economic conditions in the United States. We will therefore attempt to determine the empirical relationship between the consumption of tourist services in Jamaica and Barbados (as measured by the volume of tourist expenditures in those countries) and economic conditions in the United States (as measured by personal disposable income in both current and constant prices).

RESULTS OF REGRESSION ANALYSIS

Table B.1 shows the results of the regression analysis based on the logarithmic transformation of the simple equation model $Y = aX^b$. Thus the regression coefficient for each equation is also the elasticity coefficient. The dependent variables for each country are total tourist expenditures and the number of stopover tourists. These were regressed separately on the two independent variables—U.S. per capita disposable income in current dollars, and U.S. per capita disposable income in 1972 dollars.

The results show the following:

for both countries, tourist expenditures and the number of stopover tourists were
    generally income elastic;
the real income (in 1972 dollars) elasticities for both countries were two to three
    times larger than the current income elasticities; and
all the income elasticities for Barbados were higher than those for Jamaica.

The higher income elasticities for Barbados suggest that the growth of U.S. disposable income over the period had a greater impact on the Barbados tourist industry than on Jamaica's. Since this analysis uses annual data covering an 11-year period, it is necessarily concerned with long-run growth rather than short-run fluctuations. However, the higher income elasticities for Barbados also

TABLE B.1

Income Elasticity of Tourist Expenditures and the Number of Stopover Tourists, 1965–75

	Dependent Variables	
Independent Variables	Number of Stopover Tourists	Tourist Expenditures
	Jamaica	
U.S. per capita disposable income in current dollars	.956 (8.587)* $R^2 = .89$	1.52 (8.94) $R^2 = .88$
U.S. per capita disposable income in 1972 dollars	3.265 (11.409) $R^2 = .93$	4.217 (16.069) $R^2 = .96$
	Barbados	
U.S. per capita disposable income in current dollars	1.749 (8.743) $R^2 = .89$	2.55 (22.16) $R^2 = .98$
U.S. per capita disposable income in 1972 dollars	5.048 (16.831) $R^2 = .96$	6.106 (11.696) $R^2 = .93$

*Numbers in parentheses are t-values. For Barbados, the regression data for stopover tourists are for 1964–75; the tourist expenditures data are for 1964–74. For Jamaica, the regression data for stopover tourists are for 1965–75, while the data for tourist expenditures are for 1964–75.

Sources: Computations are based on data in Tables 3.13 and D.20.

suggest that it is more vulnerable to economic fluctuations in the United States.* The fact that the Barbadian tourist industry is smaller than that of Jamaica, and that its growth has been to some degree at the expense of the Jamaican industry (due to uncertain political conditions in Jamaica) may help to explain the higher income elasticities for Barbados.

IMPLICATIONS FOR THE FUTURE OF THE TOURIST INDUSTRY

Projected Growth of Tourists and Tourist Expenditures

Based upon the results of the above regression analysis, a forecast of the number of stopover tourists and their expenditures is possible on the assumption that the income elasticities derived for the period 1965 to 1975 are useful indicators of the volume of tourists and their expenditures over the next decade.

Between 1965 and 1975, U.S. per capita disposable income in 1972 dollars grew at an annual rate of 2.5 percent. In view of the projected decline in the growth rate of the U.S. GNP in the early 1980s to 3.2 percent,[1] it is not unrealistic to assume a growth rate for per capita disposable personal income in 1972 dollars of 2 percent.

On the basis of our estimated elasticity coefficients, a 2 percent growth in per capita disposable income in 1972 dollars would cause tourist expenditures in Jamaica to grow at an annual rate of 8.4 percent, and the number of stopover tourists by 6.4 percent. In Barbados, these growth rates would be 12.2 percent and 10.0 percent, respectively. No one expects these rates to continue ad infinitum. Indeed, political and social considerations may dictate that the scale of the industry be limited to avoid undesirable social costs.

The question of scale may very well rest upon what each country regards as an optimum ratio of tourists to total population. Peter Gray calls this ratio "tourism density" and hypothesizes that there is a positive relationship between tourism density and hostility toward tourists by the local population.[2] The implication of this hypothesis is that there is some optimum level of tourism density which maximizes the flow of tourist expenditures into local development on the one hand and minimizes hostility of residents toward tourists on the other. But the problem is far more complicated, for it encompasses such issues as: the wisdom of allocating scarce resources away from other socially desirable projects

---

*Although in 1975 only 24.7 percent of Barbados's tourists came from the United States, 58.7 percent came from North America. The Canadian economy is directly affected by U.S. economic fluctuations. Thus U.S. economic indexes in this analysis are assumed to reflect the general behavior of the North American economy.

for tourist development; the impact of tourist density on indigenous culture and art; and the strain on irreplaceable national resources which the growth of tourism may impose. These considerations must act as major constraints on the growth of the industry.

Some indication of how tourism density will behave in Jamaica and Barbados by 1985 is shown in the following projections. No consideration is given here to the geographical distribution of tourists within the two countries. If the growth of the tourist population and related activities takes place outside the densely populated urban centers, the average density ratios may very well overstate the extent to which the tourist population is visible to the local population.

In 1975 the population of Barbados was 255,000. The total number of tourist arrivals that year was 221,500, each staying an average of 8.3 days. This averages out to approximately 5,000 tourists in Barbados each day and gives a population to tourist ratio of 51:1. Jamaica, with a population of a little over 2 million, hosted 396,000 stopover tourists, each staying an average of 8.8 nights, for an average of approximately 9,500 tourists each day, yielding a density ratio of roughly 210:1. The simple density hostility hypothesis would suggest greater hostility to tourists in Barbados than in Jamaica and is thus unable to explain the cynical attitude toward tourism in Jamaica, a country undergoing important changes in social, political, and economic priorities.

Whether or not the changing priorities in Jamaica will permit the number of stopover tourists to grow at the projected rate of 6.4 percent per year is a question for the policy makers. If that projected rate of growth materializes and if the average length of stay remains at its 1975 level of 8.8 nights, then by 1985 approximately 736,000 tourists will visit Jamaica. If the Jamaican population continues to grow at its 1965–75 rate of 1.7 percent a year, by 1985 it will be 2.4 million and the tourism density will be 133:1. Likewise, if we assume that the Barbados population continues to grow at its 1965–75 rate of 0.8 percent a year, by 1985 it will be approximately 276,000. If the number of stopover tourists grows at 10 percent a year, by 1985 it will reach 575,000. Assuming their average length of stay in Barbados remains at the 1975 level of 8.3 days, by 1985 the tourist density will be 19.5:1.

Capital Requirements

To estimate the capital requirements for Jamaica, we start from 1975 when there were 22,219 beds in hotels, guest houses, resort cottages, and apartments, and a room occupancy rate of 43.5 percent and falling.[3] For the purpose of our projection, we assume that a desirable occupancy rate is 75 percent. With a projection of 18,000 tourists per day by 1985, this occupancy rate requires a minimum of 24,000 beds, or 2,000 additional beds over the 1975 level. For Barbados, based on the same 75 percent occupancy rate assumption, 17,000 beds will be required—an addition of 7,000 beds over the 1975 level. If we use the 1975 hotel bed:room ratio of 2:1 for Jamaica as a general guide to the number of additional rooms required in all types of tourist accommodations, then only 1,000 additional rooms will be required for Jamaica and 3,500 for Barbados. At an estimated construction cost per room of $25,000, the total investment required for Jamaica is $25 million, and $87.5 million for Barbados.[4]

The allocation of scarce capital resources to finance the expansion of the industry is critical, especially in the face of changing social priorities which require expanded public investment in such areas as education, housing, and health, the returns from which are not in the near term. The decision is made more difficult if the government insists on ownership participation in the industry. Under this strategy, the expansion of the industry is constrained by the government's ability not only to finance related infrastructural development but its share of the enterprise as well.

Potential Real Impact of Tourist Growth

The reduction of the import content of tourist expenditures and the expansion of tourist-generated employment are two important objectives of the expansion of the industry. But this will depend upon the development of links within the local economy as well as on the stability of domestic prices. An increase in the local supply of food and other products to the industry will reduce the industry's traditional high import content. The extent to which the domestic output is increased to meet the expanding tourist demand will in large measure determine the behavior of real tourist spending. Between 1965 and 1975, the consumer price index in Jamaica grew at an average annual rate of 10 percent. For the period between 1965 and 1972 the inflation rate was a mere 6 percent, but between 1972 and 1975 it accelerated to 21 percent due to sharp increases in the foreign prices of imported commodities and the rapid expansion of government consumption spending. For Barbados, the average annual inflation rate for the 1965–75 period was 12.1 percent. Between 1965 and 1972 it was 7.2 percent; and between 1972 and 1975 it jumped to over 24 percent.

On the assumption that tourist expenditures grow at 8.9 percent a year over the next ten years, and that the average annual inflation rate of 10 percent over the 1965–75 period is sustained over the 1975–85 period, real tourist expenditure in Jamaica will decline at a rate of 1–2 percent a year. To bring domestic inflation below 8 percent a year over the next ten years will be a major undertaking, especially in view of the extraordinary high rates experienced between 1972 and 1975. If Barbados maintains its 1965–75 inflation rate, it would just be able to keep real aggregate tourist spending constant, since tourist expenditures are projected to grow at 12.2 percent. The problem of inflation is a particularly difficult one for these small open Caribbean economies, especially because a large share of it is transmitted through international prices that these countries are in no position to influence.

NOTES

1. Joint Economic Committee, Congress of the United States, *Achieving Price Stability through Economic Growth* (Washington, D.C.: Government Printing Office, 1974), p. 13.

2. H. Peter Gray, "Towards an Economic Analysis of Tourism Policy," *Social and Economic Studies* 23 (1974): 386–97.

3. Jamaica, *Economic and Social Survey Jamaica 1975* (Kingston: The Government Printer, 1976), p. 170.

4. The estimate of $25,000 was taken from Checchi and Company, *A Plan for Managing the Growth of Tourism in the Commonwealth of the Bahama Islands* (Washington, D.C., 1969), p. 410. It applies to hotel rooms as opposed to condominiums and cottages, which were estimated at $40,000 and $20,000 per room, respectively, for the period 1970–74. Investment in supporting facilities such as transportation, restaurants, recreation, and the infrastructural investment (services, roads, communications, and so forth) that the growth of the tourist population would entail could easily double the estimated investment for accommodations alone. If the government insists on joint venturing to carry out this expansion, then we may presume that in addition to infrastructural investment, a substantial share of the expansion will be financed with public funds.

Appendix C

An Empirical Analysis of Caribbean Migration to the United States

A THEORETICAL FRAMEWORK

We will argue in this appendix that the flow of immigrants from the Caribbean (the sending country) to the United States (the reciving country) is a function of the economic differential between the two countries and the rate of unemployment in the United States.

At any given point in time, the supply of Caribbean immigrant labor is greater than the U.S. demand for it. That is to say, more workers would like to migrate to the United States than the number to whom immigrant visas are issued. The reasons cover a wide range of push-pull factors. Principal among them are the U.S. unemployment rate and the wide income differential between the United States and the Caribbean—a differential that is thoroughly familiar to potential immigrants because it has been widely demonstrated through the tourist industry, various forms of communications and entertainment, and through Caribbean expatriates who live in the United States. Income differential is a combination of push-pull factors since the extent of the differential is determined by income determinants in the sending country as well as in the receiving country. The rate of unemployment in the United States is a pull factor since it indicates the extent to which employment opportunities are available in the United States.

Given: the wide disparity between income opportunities between the Caribbean and the United States; the proximity of the Caribbean to the United States; the high degree of knowledge about conditions in the United States; and the propensity of the Caribbean worker to migrate to developed urban metropolitan areas, we will argue that the number of immigrant visas issued will depend upon economic conditions in the United States. This is not to suggest that there is an explicit visa-issuing policy that is directly keyed to the level of economic activity in the United States. We are merely hypothesizing that the number of immigrant visas issued to immigrant workers from the Caribbean between 1965 and 1975 is not unrelated to the rate of unemployment in the United States.

During periods of high (or full) employment in the United States, the country will generally increase its imports of both goods and labor from the Caribbean as well as from other nations. This creates fundamental conflicts in the supplying country. If we assume, for example, that the typical worker who was issued an immigrant visa to the United States was employed in his home country, some output is foregone when he emigrated, if he was not immediately replaced either by another worker or by capital equipment. If the emigrant worker were skilled, it would take some time to replace him, especially where there is a scarcity of such workers. If he were semiskilled or unskilled, he would be quickly replaced. But even if he were replaced immediately, some inefficiency would result for a while because his replacement would probably have less experience. Thus if the emigration rate from the Caribbean increased at a time when there was an increase in the external demand for Caribbean goods, some of the gains from the growth of exports would be offset by output foregone. Further, if Caribbean employers expected prosperity in the United States to increase the rate of Caribbean emigration, they might very well choose to increase the capital intensity of their production process as a hedge against further increases in the rate of emigration. Such a move would tend to operate against the development of labor-intensive industries.

Given the elasticity of the rate of emigration with respect to the wage differential between the sending country and the receiving country (curves E^1, E^2, and E^3 in Figure C.1), the rate of emigration from the sending country at any point in time will be influenced by the rate of unemployment in the receiving country. On the other hand, the impact of a shift in the unemployment isoquant, U, on the rate of emigration from the sending country will depend on the elasticity of the emigration curve, E, and the shape and position of the unemployment isoquant, U. Where there is a wide income differential between the sending and receiving countries, the elasticity of the rate of emigration is assumed to be low, as indicated by the emigration curve E^1; it is also assumed that the emigration rate will generally be high. Over time as income differential declines, the rate of emigration will generally tend to decline and to become more sensitive to small changes in income differential. Thus a long-run emigration curve $GONE^1$ could be drawn (as in Figure C.1) from the short-run emigration curves E^1, E^2, and E^3. The response of the rate of emigration to changes in the rate of unemployment in the receiving country would vary depending upon the elasticity of the emigration curve facing the sending country. The higher the elasticity of the emigration curve, the greater the impact of the unemployment rate in the receiving country on the rate of emigration from the sending country.

While income differential determines the slope of the short-run emigration curve, other factors such as the proximity to the receiving country, information about the receiving country, and the stock of expatriates from the sending country now living in the receiving country determine its position.

It may seem paradoxical that the rate of emigration from a developing country (with an inelastic emigration curve) is less influenced by the unemployment rate in the receiving developed country than is the rate of emigration from a developed country (with an elastic emigration curve). Perhaps the explanation lies in the fact that in developed countries where labor is generally more skilled and therefore more productive, it tends to be more mobile and therefore more responsive to changes in wage differentials. However, it is important to understand that as the rate of emigration becomes more responsive to changes in income differential and unemployment rates in the receiving country, the absolute rate of emigration tends to decline in the long run. Thus as we move from right to left on the long-run emigration curve, $GONE^1$, in Figure C.1, the elasticity increases and the absolute rate of emigration declines. Each segment of the long-run emigration curve implies a particular stage of development of the sending country as well as a maximum absolute rate of emigration. Because the

FIGURE C.1

Short- and Long-Run Emigration Curves

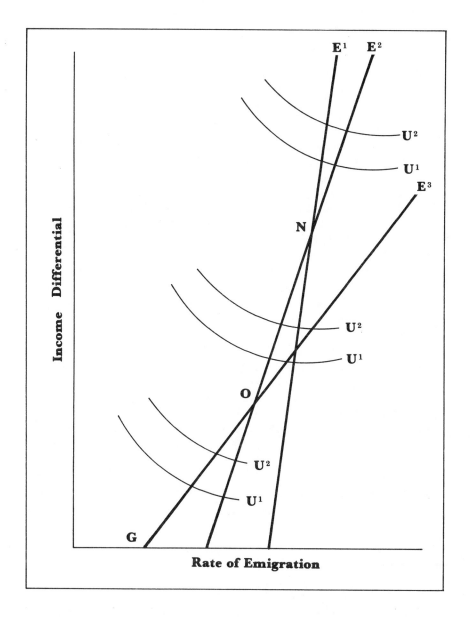

Source: Constructed by the author.

long-run emigration curve is derived from three short-run curves, it shows three distinct elasticity segments corresponding to three stages of development. If at each stage of development the sending country is faced with the same set of unemployment isoquants, it follows that the influence of the receiving country unemployment rate on the rate of emigration becomes larger as development takes place, that is, as the income differential declines.* Note that even if the income differential is reduced to zero in the long run, the rate of emigration would still be positive.

POLICY IMPLICATIONS

The preceding hypothesis that as income differential declines, the rate of emigration from the sending country will decline even though the responsiveness of the rate of emigration to small changes in income differential and to changes in the receiving country unemployment rates increase implies that if both receiving and sending countries wish to reduce the rate of emigration from the sending country, efforts must be directed toward the long-run solution of reducing the income differential between the two countries. The effect of short-run measures will necessarily be limited since these measures are not likely to have any major impact on the income differential, especially in the case where the rate of emigration with respect to changes in the income differential is inelastic in the short run. Short-term measures which do little to address the fundamental problem of scarcity of economic opportunities in the sending country, and the wide income differential between the sending and receiving countries, will cause the rate of emigration to move along the E^1 curve in Figure C.1. The net effect is that the rate of emigration will not change very much unless repressive measures are implemented by the receiving country to shift the E^1 curve to the left. This approach is likely to create serious international political problems which may very well dwarf the problems they were intended to solve.

A rational approach to the problem would require the receiving country to assist the sending country through a wide range of programs to accelerate its rate of economic development, thereby reducing the wide income differential which combines powerful push and pull factors. Thus the phenomenon of international migration from developing to developed countries demands international cooperation to remedy glaring imbalances between the well-being of peoples of the sending and the receiving countries.

---

*A shift of the unemployment isoquant from U^1 to U^2 means a reduction in the rate of unemployment (or an increase in the rate of employment).

EMPIRICAL ANALYSIS

We have hypothesized that the rate of emigration is a function of the income differential between the sending and the receiving countries and the rate of unemployment in the receiving country. Table C.1 provides the relevant data for Jamaica and the United States.

The variables are defined as follows:

M_L = rate of emigration from the Jamaican labor force;

M_{PTK} = rate of emigration from professional, technical, and kindred occupations in Jamaica;

P_o = income differential (the ratio of per capita output of the labor force in Jamaica to per capita output of the civilian labor force in the United States);

U_r = the unemployment rate in the United States.

TABLE C.1

Data for Regression Analysis

Year	M_L	M_{PTK}	P_o	U_r
1963	0.16	0.96	12.48	5.7
1964	0.15	0.89	12.72	5.2
1965	0.13	0.62	12.72	4.5
1966	0.22	1.30	12.60	3.8
1967	1.14	4.80	12.96	3.8
1968	1.98	6.31	13.08	3.6
1969	1.68	5.53	13.56	3.5
1970	1.13	3.54	14.40	4.9
1971	1.01	3.17	14.52	5.9
1972	0.87	2.22	15.00	5.6
1973	0.56	1.58	17.00	4.9
1974	0.65	1.45	20.60	5.6
1975	0.56	1.09	21.60	8.5
1976	0.46	1.11	19.90	7.7

Source: R. W. Palmer, "A Decade of West Indian Migration to the United States, 1962–1972: An Economic Analysis", *Social and Economic Studies* 23 (1974): 571–87; *Economic Report of the President 1977* (Washington, D.C.: Government Printing Office, 1978) *Economic and Social Surveys Jamaica 1973–76* (Kingston: Government Printer, 1974–1977) U.S. Immigration and Naturalization Service, *Annual Reports*, 1973–76 (Washington, D.C.: Government Printing Office, 1974–77).

TABLE C.2

Results of Regression Analysis

	1963–76	1968–76
1. a. M_L	$= 1.098 - 0.0219P_o$ $(.430)^*$ $R^2 = .01$	$= 3.163 - 0.1308P_o$ (3.585) $R^2 = .33$
b. M_{PTK}	$= 5.434 - 0.1947P_o$ (1.221) $R^2 = .11$	$= 11.153 - 0.4973P_o$ (4.044) $R^2 = .70$
2. a. M_L	$= 1.586 - 0.1572U_r$ (1.526) $R^2 = .16$	$= 2.384 - 0.2502U_r$ (3.3711) $R^2 = .61$
b. M_{PTK}	$= 6.258 - 0.7246U_r$ (2.373) $R^2 = .31$	$= 8.001 - 0.9327U_r$ (3.610) $R^2 = .65$
3. a. M_L	$= 1.0563 + 0.08203P_o - 0.2948U_r$ $(1.129) \quad (1.857)$ $R^2 = .24$	$= 2.9984 - 0.0791P_o - 0.1242U_r$ $(1.264) \quad (1.014)$ $R^2 = .69$
b. M_{PTK}	$= 5.319 + 0.1460P_o - 0.9703U_r$ $(.653) \quad (1.983)$ $R^2 = .34$	$= 10.5198 - 0.3133P_o - 0.4338U_r$ $(1.498) \quad (1.060)$ $R^2 = .74$

*t-values are in parentheses.

Source: Computations are based on the data in Table C.1.

Three sets of ordinary least-squares regressions were run using two separate dependent variables (M_L and M_{PTK}) in each set for the periods 1963–76 and 1968–76. The 1963–76 period represents the postindependence years as well as the period after British restriction on immigrants from the Caribbean. The 1968–76 period is the time of large-scale emigration to the United States. The results are shown in Table C.2.

The results indicate that changes in income differential (P_o) (as defined for this analysis) over the 13-year period from 1963 to 1976 explain very little of the variations in the rate of emigration, whether from the labor force as a whole or from the professional and technical occupations. The fact is that although there were marginal changes in income differential, the income gap remained wide. And for each group of emigrants, marginal changes had little or no effect on their decision to emigrate. For the professional and technical group, income differential had a slight influence on the rate of emigration. The sign for the coefficient of the income differential was negative as expected, indicating that the smaller the income differential (the larger P_o gets), the smaller the rate of emigration.

The rate of unemployment in the United States (U_r) was a stronger influence on the rate of emigration, especially emigration from the professional and technical occupations. The unemployment coefficients are negative as was expected, indicating that an increase in U.S. unemployment rates will reduce the rate of emigration from Jamaica. In equation 3a, P_o and U_r are shown to explain some 24 percent of the variation in the rate of emigration from the labor force and 34 percent of the variation in the rate of emigration from the professional, technical, and kindred occupations. The sign for the P_o coefficient, however, has turned positive, suggesting that there is some interaction between P_o and U_r. The regression results for the 1968–76 period show markedly higher R^2s and generally higher levels of significance for the regression coefficients in all equations.

The conclusion of a U.S. Department of Labor study that "the number [of immigrant workers] has been roughly the same, year after year, and hence does not reflect increases and decreases in the unemployment rate,"[1] does not necessarily conflict with our results since population growth will cause the rate of emigration to decline if the number of emigrants remains stable. However, in the Jamaican case, the decline in the rate of emigration since 1968 was the result of factors other than population growth.

NOTE

1. U.S. Department of Labor, *Immigrants and the American Labor Market*, Manpower Research Monograph No. 31 (Washington, D.C.: Government Printing Office, 1974), p. 47.

Appendix D
Selected Statistical Data

TABLE D.1

Imports and Exports as a Percent of Gross Domestic Product, 1970 and 1975

Country	Imports, Percent GDP		Exports, Percent GDP		Imports + Exports, Percent GDP	
	1970	1975	1970	1975	1970	1975
Barbados	77.6	62.5	27.3	31.0	104.9	93.5
Guyana	50.0	68.0	49.8	70.7	99.8	138.7
Jamaica	36.6	38.4	23.8	26.8	60.4	65.2
Trinidad and Tobago	62.4	65.4	55.1	78.2	117.5	143.6

Source: International Monetary Fund, *International Financial Statistics*.

TABLE D.2

Percentage Distribution of Imports by Economic Functions or End Use, 1974

Item	Jamaica	Guyana	Trinidad and Tobago*
Consumer goods	22.0	24.9	29.1
Raw materials and intermediate goods	51.0	48.7	57.8
Capital goods	27.0	26.4	22.2

*Figures are for 1975.

Sources: Central Bank of Trinidad and Tobago, *Statistical Digest*, June 1977; *Economic Survey of Guyana* (Georgetown: Ministry of Economic Development, 1974); *Economic and Social Survey Jamaica 1975* (Kingston: The Government Printer, 1976).

TABLE D.3

Bauxite and Alumina Exports from Jamaica, 1955–76
(J $ thousand)

Year	Bauxite	Alumina	Total
1955	7,768	9,568	17,336
1956	9,200	11,606	20,806
1957	19,126	23,822	42,948
1958	25,194	18,264	43,458
1959	22,032	18,812	40,844
1960	21,774	33,268	55,042
1961	26,118	33,770	59,888
1962	31,430	28,846	60,276
1963	27,100	31,902	59,002
1964	31,328	36,368	67,696
1965	35,618	34,986	70,604
1966	70,196	38,634	108,830
1967	71,420	41,772	113,196
1968	62,120	50,833	112,953
1969	76,010	69,830	145,840
1970	75,452	111,141	186,893
1971	74,630	104,316	178,946
1972	68,375	119,867	188,242
1973	79,584	147,769	129,353
1974	134,745	346,733	481,478
1975	98,109	303,859	401,968
1976	112,649	276,774	389,423

Source: *Economic and Social Survey Jamaica* (Kingston: The Government Printer).

TABLE D.4

Bauxite and Alumina Exports from Guyana, 1961–75
(G $ million)

Year	Bauxite	Alumina	Total
1961	28.5	12.1	40.6
1962	31.1	22.7	53.8
1963	25.7	22.3	48.0
1964	30.2	26.7	56.9
1965	37.4	30.5	67.9
1966	46.3	33.1	79.4
1967	51.5	31.3	82.8
1968	67.2	33.0	100.2
1969	78.8	41.5	120.3
1970	92.1	46.4	138.5
1971	96.0	40.5	136.5
1972	102.2	29.0	131.2
1973	107.4	26.9	134.3
1974	152.7	46.4	199.1
1975	198.6	65.5	264.1

Source: Annual Statistical Abstract, 1974 (Georgetown: Ministry of Economic Development, 1975); International Monetary Fund, *International Financial Statistics.*

TABLE D.5

Population of the Caribbean, 1962–76
(in thousands)

Year	Barbados	Guyana	Jamaica	Trinidad	Total
1962	232.9	595.0	1,625.7	900.5	3,354.1
1963	233.3	609.0	1,664.8	924.2	3,431.3
1964	233.6	624.0	1,701.7	951.1	3,510.4
1965	234.0	639.0	1,747.3	973.9	3,594.2
1966	234.4	654.0	1,788.0	994.8	3,671.2
1967	234.7	670.0	1,811.2	1,010.1	3,726.0
1968	235.1	686.0	1,831.0	1,020.6	3,772.7
1969	235.5	702.0	1,855.5	1,027.8	3,820.8
1970	235.9	714.0	1,880.0	1,026.7	3,856.6
1971	237.0	736.0	1,895.4	1,032.5	3,900.9
1972	241.7	754.0	1,930.8	1,048.4	3,974.9
1973	247.5	772.0	1,991.0	1,061.8	4,072.3
1974	251.2	779.0	2,025.0	1,066.0	4,121.2
1975	254.8	785.0	2,060.3	1,148.6	4,248.7
1976	258.5	800.0	2,084.2	1,170.3	4,313.0

Sources: International Bank for Reconstruction and Development, *World Tables, 1974* (Washington, D.C.: IBRD, 1977); Barbados, *Monthly Digest of Statistics* (Bridgetown: Statistical Service, 1977); *Economic and Social Survey Jamaica 1970 to 1975* (Kingston: The Government Printer, 1971 to 1976); International Monetary Fund, *International Financial Statistics*; Trinidad and Tobago, *Annual Statistical Digest 1973–74* (Port-of-Spain: Central Statistical Office, 1975).

TABLE D.6

Migration from Jamaica to the United States as a Percent of Total Migration to North America and the United Kingdom, 1962–75

Year	United States	Canada	United Kingdom	Total	United States as Percent of Total
1962	1,573	488*	22,779	24,840	6.3
1963	1,880	735*	7,494	10,109	18.5
1964	1,762	726*	9,560	12,048	14.6
1965	1,837	1,214	9,510	12,561	14.6
1966	2,743	1,407	7,077	11,227	24.4
1967	10,483	3,459	8,107	22,049	47.5
1968	17,470	2,886	4,640	24,996	69.9
1969	16,947	3,889	2,699	23,535	72.0
1970	15,033	4,659	2,372	22,064	68.1
1971	14,571	3,903	1,759	20,233	72.0
1972	13,427	3,092	1,620	18,139	74.0
1973	9,963	9,363	1,872	21,198	47.0
1974	12,408	11,286	1,397	25,091	49.4
1975	11,076	8,211	1,394	20,681	53.5

*According to George Roberts, direct emigration from the West Indies to Canada in 1965 was 3,665 ("A Note on Recent Migration from the West Indies to Canada," in *West Indies-Canada Economic Relations*, [Kingston: Institute for Social and Economic Research, University of the West Indies, 1967], pp. 62–74). Since the number of Jamaicans emigrating to Canada that year was 1,214, or 33 percent of the total, the number of Jamaicans emigrating to Canada for 1962, 1963, and 1964 was assumed to be the same percentage of total West Indies migration to Canada provided by Roberts for those years.

Sources: *Economic and Social Survey Jamaica* (Kingston: The Government Printer); U.S. Immigration and Naturalization Service, *Annual Reports 1962–76* (Washington, D.C.: Government Printing Office, 1963–77).

TABLE D.7

Migration of Physicians, Surgeons, and Dentists, 1962–76

Year	Jamaica	Trinidad and Tobago	Barbados	Guyana	Total
1962	47	1	0	0	48
1963	9	1	1	4	15
1964	8	5	0	8	21
1965	3	8	1	2	14
1966	15	6	0	3	24
1967	27	11	2	1	41
1968	20	7	1	6	34
1969	20	6	2	0	28
1970	14	6	0	11	31
1971	31	11	2	9	53
1972	24	17	1	14	56
1973	22	12	6	5	45
1974	36	16	1	18	71
1975	29	8	12	4	53
1976	39	15	6	8	68
1962–76	344	130	35	93	602

Source: U.S. Immigration and Naturalization Service.

TABLE D.8

Migration of Engineers, 1962–76

Year	Jamaica	Trinidad and Tobago	Barbados	Guyana	Total
1962	33	4	3	1	41
1963	22	7	3	3	35
1964	21	6	3	2	32
1965	12	8	2	3	25
1966	24	7	1	2	34
1967	52	19	4	9	84
1968	67	23	7	7	104
1969	50	24	11	8	93
1970	31	22	10	7	70
1971	38	26	10	13	87
1972	30	18	5	18	71
1973	24	12	6	5	47
1974	24	22	5	16	67
1975	27	14	10	14	65
1976	35	13	8	19	75
1962 –76	490	225	88	127	930

Source: U.S Immigration and Naturalization Service.

TABLE D.9

Migration of Nurses to the United States, 1962–76
(fiscal years ending June 30)

Year	Jamaica	Trinidad	Barbados	Guyana	Total
1962	42	34	13	23	112
1963	74	36	13	38	161
1964	64	16	13	23	116
1965	40	18	17	16	91
1966	115	47	23	35	220
1967	533	132	23	77	765
1968	785	197	62	105	1,149
1969	564	199	81	128	972
1970	253	132	54	103	542
1971	246	124	50	142	562
1972	187	87	23	75	372
1973	114	65	7	89	275
1974	105	45	18	40	208
1975	94	52	30	33	209
1976	94	54	19	40	207
1962 –76	3,310	1,238	446	967	5,961

Source: U.S. Immigration and Naturalization Service.

TABLE D.10

Impact of Migration to the United States on the Population Growth of Trinidad and Tobago, 1962-75

Year	Natural Increase	Migration to the United States	Migration to the United States as a Percent of Natural Increase
1962	27,735	388	1.4
1963	26,428	448	1.7
1964	26,345	413	1.5
1965	25,222	485	1.9
1966	23,019	756	3.3
1967	21,687	2,160	9.9
1968	20,991	5,266	25.0
1969	18,062	6,835	37.8
1970	18,195	7,350	40.4
1971	19,072	7,130	37.4
1972	21,094	6,615	31.3
1973	21,008	7,035	33.5
1974	18,633	6,516	34.9
1975	18,056	5,982	33.1
1962-75	305,547	57,379	18.8

Sources: U.S. Immigration and Naturalization Service, *Annual Reports 1962-76* (Washington, D.C.: Government Printing Office, 1963-77); Trinidad and Tobago, *Third Five-Year Plan 1969-1973 (Draft)* (Port-of-Spain: Government Printery, 1969); and *Annual Statistical Digest 1973-74* (Port-of-Spain: Central Statistical Office, 1975).

TABLE D.11

Impact of Migration to the United States on the Population Growth of Jamaica, 1962–75

Year	Natural Increase	Migration to the United States	Migration to the United States as a Percent of Natural Increase
1962	52,104	1,573	3.0
1963	51,518	1,880	3.6
1964	55,790	1,762	3.1
1965	55,684	1,837	3.3
1966	57,076	2,743	4.8
1967	54,143	10,483	19.3
1968	50,845	17,470	34.3
1969	50,574	16,947	33.5
1970	50,023	15,033	30.0
1971	52,199	14,571	27.9
1972	52,249	13,427	25.7
1973	47,700	9,963	20.8
1974	47,100	12,408	26.3
1975	47,400	11,076	23.4
1962–75	724,405	131,173	18.1

Sources: *Economic and Social Surveys Jamaica* (Kingston: The Government Printer); U.S. Immigration and Naturalization Service, *Annual Reports 1962–76* (Washington, D.C.: Government Printing Office, 1963–77).

TABLE D.12

Impact of Migration to the United States on the Population Growth of Guyana, 1962–75

Year	Natural Increase	Migration to the United States	Migration to the United States as a Percent of Natural Increase
1962	19,620	268	1.3
1963	19,393	273	1.4
1964	18,767	296	1.5
1965	18,130	233	1.3
1966	20,119	377	1.8
1967	18,848	857	4.5
1968	19,464	1,148	5.9
1969	18,095	1,615	8.9
1970	19,186	1,763	9.2
1971	19,930*	2,115	10.6
1972	20,961*	2,826	13.5
1973	21,461*	2,969	13.8
1974	21,656*	3,241	14.9
1975	21,823*	3,169	14.5
1962–75	277,453	21,150	7.6

*Estimate based on the average of 27.8 per thousand for 1968–70.

Sources: Economic Survey of Guyana, 1966 (Georgetown: Ministry of Economic Development, 1967); U.S. Immigration and Naturalization Service, *Annual Reports 1962–76* (Washington, D.C.: Government Printing Office, 1963–77); Guyana, *Annual Statistical Abstract, 1974* (Georgetown: Ministry of Economic Development, 1975).

TABLE D.13

Impact of Migration to the United States on the Population Growth of Barbados, 1962–75

Year	Natural Increase	Migration to the United States	Migration to the United States as a Percent of Natural Increase
1962	4,765	406	8.5
1963	4,793	376	7.8
1964	4,379	393	8.9
1965	4,453	406	9.1
1966	4,307	520	12.0
1967	3,408	1,037	30.4
1968	3,429	2,024	59.0
1969	3,221	1,957	60.7
1970	2,819	1,774	62.9
1971	3,138	1,731	55.1
1972	3,258	1,620	49.7
1973	2,797	1,448	51.7
1974	2,744	1,461	53.2
1975	2,687	1,618	60.2
1962–75	50,198	16,771	33.4

Sources: Barbados, *Monthly Digest of Statistics* (Bridgetown: Statistical Service, 1977), *Economic Survey 1968; 1971* (Bridgetown: Economic Planning Unit, 1969, 1972); U.S. Immigration and Naturalization Service, *Annual Reports 1962–76* (Washington, D.C.: Government Printing Office, 1963–77).

TABLE D.14

Index of Money Supply, 1965–75
(1965 = 100.0)

Year	Jamaica	Trinidad and Tobago	Guyana	Barbados
1965	100.0	100.0	100.0	100.0
1966	113.8	107.8	108.5	128.7
1967	116.0	113.2	122.1	136.2
1968	146.1	114.5	137.8	157.6
1969	170.4	121.6	150.8	183.3
1970	194.6	141.3	161.9	205.5
1971	245.6	171.5	188.9	205.2
1972	264.9	205.0	227.3	229.5
1973	319.2	194.9	190.0	236.8
1974	393.3	255.6	279.7	254.9
1975	481.2	371.6	361.6	317.5

Sources: *Economic and Social Survey Jamaica 1970 to 1975* (Kingston: The Government Printer, 1971 to 1976); Barbados, *Monthly Digest of Statistics* (Bridgetown: Statistical Service, 1977); Trinidad and Tobago, *Annual-Statistical Digest 1973–74* (Port-of-Spain: Central Statistical Office, 1975); Guyana, *Economic Bulletin* (Georgetown: Bank of Guyana, 1976), and *Annual Statistical Abstract, 1974* (Georgetown: Ministry of Economic Development, 1975); Trinidad and Tobago, *Quarterly Economic Report April–June 1976* (Port-of-Spain: Central Statistical Office, 1976).

TABLE D.15

Index of Consumer Prices, 1965-75
(1965 = 100.0)

Year	Jamaica	Trinidad and Tobago	Guyana	Barbados
1965	100.0	100.0	100.0	100.0
1966	102.2	115.5	102.1	102.1
1967	104.2	118.0	105.2	105.9
1968	111.6	127.6	108.4	114.4
1969	117.2	130.8	109.9	120.0
1970	130.1	134.1	113.6	129.6
1971	138.7	138.8	114.7	139.6
1972	146.9	151.7	120.5	155.8
1973	175.1	174.2	129.6	180.9
1974	222.6	212.5	152.1	251.3
1975	‐261.4	231.8	164.3	302.3

Sources: Economic and Social Survey Jamaica 1970 to 1975 (Kingston: The Government Printer, 1971 to 1976); Barbados, *Monthly Digest of Statistics* (Bridgetown: Statistical Service, 1977); Trinidad and Tobago, *Annual-Statistical Digest 1973-74* (Port-of-Spain: Central Statistical Office, 1975); Guyana, *Economic Bulletin* (Georgetown: Bank of Guyana, 1976), and *Annual Statistical Abstract, 1974* (Georgetown: Ministry of Economic Development, 1975); Trinidad and Tobago, *Quarterly Economic Report April-June 1976* (Port-of-Spain: Central Statistical Office, 1976).

TABLE D.16

Index of Import Prices, 1965–75
(1965 = 100.0)

Year	Jamaica	Trinidad and Tobago	Guyana	Barbados
1965	100.0	100.0	100.0	100.0
1966	104.0	108.1	102.1	112.8
1967	107.1	116.2	104.9	115.3
1968	122.2	135.2	106.3	144.5
1969	124.0	141.1	111.3	146.2
1970	127.8	145.6	121.6	166.2
1971	138.8	161.0	129.0	188.6
1972	145.9	175.4	151.1	199.6
1973	203.4	203.9	167.8	205.5
1974	299.5	483.6	269.1	393.9
1975	333.4	528.6	290.6	473.8

Sources: *Economic and Social Survey Jamaica 1970 to 1975* (Kingston: The Government Printer, 1971 to 1976); Barbados, *Monthly Digest of Statistics* (Bridgetown: Statistical Service, 1977); Trinidad and Tobago, *Annual-Statistical Digest 1973–74* (Port-of-Spain: Central Statistical Office, 1975); Guyana, *Economic Bulletin* (Georgetown: Bank of Guyana, 1976), and *Annual Statistical Abstract, 1974* (Georgetown: Ministry of Economic Development, 1975); Trinidad and Tobago, *Quarterly Economic Report April-June 1976* (Port-of-Spain: Central Statistical Office, 1976).

TABLE D.17

International Reserves, 1970–76
($ million)

Year	Jamaica	Guyana	Trinidad and Tobago	Barbados
1970	139.2	20.4	43.0	16.6
1971	179.0	26.1	69.4	18.8
1972	159.7	36.7	58.3	28.0
1973	127.4	13.9	47.0	32.4
1974	190.4	62.5	390.3	39.1
1975	125.6	100.5	751.0	39.6
1976	32.4	27.2	1,013.5	28.0

Source: International Monetary Fund, *International Financial Statistics*.

TABLE D.18

Claims on Governments by Monetary Authorities and the Banking System, 1970–76

Year	Monetary Authorities	Commercial Banks
	Jamaica (J $ million)	
1970	6.5	63.0
1971	10.5	76.3
1972	32.8	79.0
1973	51.4	74.2
1974	72.2	76.8
1975	181.8	106.7
1976	492.9	133.3
	Guyana (G $ million)	
1970	16.2	20.8
1971	15.3	37.6
1972	17.5	58.8
1973	84.9	66.4
1974	24.4	63.7
1975	− 3.4	136.1
1976	247.5	135.8
	Trinidad and Tobago (TT $ million)	
1970	41.2	58.3
1971	23.1	113.2
1972	66.3	98.2
1973	98.3	69.7
1974	40.9	114.7
1975	21.4	102.9
1976	− 4.6	120.2
	Barbados (B $ million)	
1970	3.80	8.00
1971	5.80	17.40
1972	5.80	19.10
1973	10.99	3.68
1974	25.76	37.10
1975	27.91	55.27
1976	37.99	76.13

Source: International Monetary Fund, *International Financial Statistics*.

TABLE D.19

United States Aluminum Production, 1955–73
($ million)

Year	Amount
1955	830.8
1956	968.8
1957	1,020.7
1958	916.7
1959	1,131.3
1960	1,201.3
1961	1,123.4
1962	1,219.0
1963	1,266.8
1964	1,455.0
1965	1,337.8
1966	1,446.0
1967	1,614.5
1968	1,639.6
1969	2,013.4
1970	2,190.0
1971	2,154.4
1972	2,084.9
1973	2,206.4

Source: U.S. Bureau of Mines, *Minerals Yearbook, 1975* (Washington, D.C.: Government Printing Office, 1976).

TABLE D.20

Per Capita Disposable Personal Income of the United States, 1964-75

Year	Current Dollars	1972 Dollars
1964	2,278	3,009
1965	2,430	3,152
1966	2,597	3,274
1967	2,740	3,371
1968	2,930	3,464
1969	3,111	3,515
1970	3,348	3,619
1971	3,588	3,714
1972	3,837	3,837
1973	4,285	4,062
1974	4,646	3,973
1975	5,077	4,014

Source: *Economic Report of the President, 1977* (Washington, D.C.: Government Printing Office, 1977).

Bibliography

BOOKS

Angelopoulos, Angelos Th. *For a New Policy of International Development*. New York: Praeger Publishers, 1977.

Avramovic, Dragoslav, and Associates. *Economic Growth and External Debt*. Baltimore: Johns Hopkins University Press, 1964.

Bird, Richard M., and Oliver Oldman, eds. *Readings on Taxation in Developing Countries*. Baltimore: Johns Hopkins University Press, 1975.

Callender, Charles V. *The Development of the Capital Market Institutions in Jamaica*. Kingston: Institute of Social and Economic Research, University of the West Indies, 1965.

Checchi and Company. *A Plan for Managing the Growth of Tourism in the Commonwealth of the Bahama Islands*. Washington, D.C.: 1969.

Committee for Economic Development. *Regional Integration and the Trade of Latin America*. New York: Committee for Economic Development, 1968.

Girvan, Norman. *The Caribbean Bauxite Industry*. Kingston: Institute for Social and Economic Research, University of the West Indies, 1967.

———, and Owen Jefferson, eds. *Readings in the Political Economy of the Caribbean*. Kingston: New World Group, 1971.

Hagelberg, G. B. *The Caribbean Sugar Industries: Constraints and Opportunities*. New Haven, Conn.: Yale University Antilles Research Program, 1974.

Hansen, Bent. *The Economic Theory of Fiscal Policy*. London: George Allen & Unwin, 1967.

Manley, Michael. *The Politics of Change: A Jamaican Testament*. Washington, D.C.: Howard University Press, 1975.

McIntyre, A., and B. Watson. *Studies in Foreign Investment in the Commonwealth Caribbean: No. 1—Trinidad and Tobago.* Kingston: Institute for Social and Economic Research, University of the West Indies, 1970.

Ohlin, Goran. *Aid and Indebtedness.* Paris: Organisation for Economic Co-operation and Development, 1966.

Peacock, Alan T., and Gerald Hauser, eds. *Government Finance and Economic Development.* Paris: Organisation for Economic Co-operation and Development, 1965.

Prachowny, Martin F. J. *Small Open Economies.* Lexington, Mass.: D. C. Heath, 1975.

Sherlock, Philip. *This is Jamaica—An Informal Guide.* London: Hodder and Stoughton, 1968.

Stone, Carl, and Aggrey Brown, eds. *Essays on Power and Change in Jamaica.* Kingston: Jamaica Publishing House, 1977.

Watson, Beverly. *Supplementary Notes on Foreign Investment in the Commonwealth Caribbean.* Kingston: Institute for Social and Economic Research, University of the West Indies, 1974.

Williams, Eric. *From Columbus to Castro: The History of the Caribbean 1492–1969.* London: Andre Deutsch, 1970.

JOURNAL ARTICLES

Abbott, George C. "Estimates of the Growth of the Population of the West Indies to 1975." *Social and Economic Studies* 12 (September 1963): 236–45.

Aronson, Robert L. "Labour Commitment Among Bauxite Workers." *Social and Economic Studies* 10 (June 1961): 156–82.

Ayub, Mahmood A., and Eric D. Cruikshank. "The Political Economy of the Caribbean." *Finance and Development* 14 (December 1977): 38–41.

Blackman, Courtney N. "Managing Reserves for Development." *The Columbia Journal of World Business* 11 (Fall 1976): 34–40.

DeWind, Josh et al. "The Cane Contract: West Indians in Florida." *NACLA Report on the Americas* 11 (November–December 1977): 11–17.

Fitzgerald, E. V. K. "Some Aspects of the Political Economy of the Latin American State." *Development and Change* 7 (April 1976): 119–33.

Flanders, M. June, and Elahanan Helpman. "On Exchange Rate Policies for a Small Country." *Economic Journal* 88 (March 1978): 44–58.

Galbraith, John Kenneth. "Power and the Useful Economist." *American Economic Review*, 63 (March 1973): 1–11.

Geiser, Hans-Joerg. "The Lomé Convention and Caribbean Integration: A First Assessment." *Revista/Review Interamericana* 6 (Spring 1976): 23–48.

Gillis, Malcolm, and Charles E. McLure. "Incidence of World Taxes on Natural Resources with Special Reference to Bauxite." *American Economic Review* 65 (May 1975): 389–96.

Girling, R. K. "The Migration of Human Capital from the Third World: The Implications and Some Data on the Jamaican Case." *Social and Economic Studies* 23 (1974): 84–96.

Grant, C. H. "Political Sequence to Alcan Nationalization in Guyana—The International Aspects." *Social and Economic Studies* 22 (June 1973): 249–71.

Grey, H. Peter. "Towards an Economic Analysis of Tourism Policy." *Social and Economic Studies* 23 (September 1974): 386–97.

Hume, Ian M. "Migrant Workers in Europe." *Finance and Development* 10 (March 1973): 2–6.

Kreinin, Mordecai E. "The Effect of Exchange Rates Changes on the Prices and Volume of Foreign Trade." *IMF Staff Papers* 24 (July 1977).

Leff, Nathaniel H. "The New Economic Order—Bad Economics, Worse Politics." *Foreign Policy*, Fall 1976, 202–17.

Lewis, W. Arthur. "The Industrialization of the British West Indies." *Caribbean Economic Review* (May 1950).

Mandle, Jay R. "Continuity and Change in Guyanese Underdevelopment." *Revista/Review Interamericana* 7 (Summer 1977): 216–26.

Mundell, R. A. "Capital Mobility and Stabilization Policy Under Fixed and Flexible Exchange Rates." *Canadian Journal of Economics and Political Science* 29 (November 1963): 475–85.

Palmer, R. W. "A Decade of West Indian Migration to the United States, 1962–1972: An Economic Analysis." *Social and Economic Studies* 23 (December 1974): 571–87.

Pinto, Aníbal, and Jan Kñakal. "The Centre-Periphery System Twenty Years Later." *Social and Economic Studies* 22 (March 1973): 34–89.

Premdas, Ralph R. "Guyana: Socialist Reconstruction or Political Opportunism?" *Journal of Interamerican Studies and World Affairs* 20 (May 1978): 133–64.

Prince, Ethlyn. "The Development of Public Enterprise in Guyana." *Social and Economic Studies* 23 (June 1974): 204–15.

Roberts, George W. "Prospects for Population Growth in the West Indies." *Social and Economic Studies* 11 (December 1962): 333–50.

———. "Provisional Assessment of Growth of the Kingston-St. Andrew Area, 1960–1970." *Social and Economic Studies* 12 (December 1963): 432–41.

Rothenberg, Jane, and Amy Wishner. "Focus on Trinidad." *NACLA's Latin America & Empire Report* 10 (October 1976): 14–30.

Sanderson, Fred A. "Export Opportunities for Agricultural Products: Implications for US Agricultural and Trade Policies." *Columbia Journal of World Business* 10 (Fall 1975): 15–28.

Sinclair, Sonia S. "A Fertility Analysis of Jamaica." *Social and Economic Studies* 23 (December 1974): 588–636.

Weeks, John. "Employment, Growth, and Foreign Domination in Underdeveloped Countries." A Warner Modular Publications Reprint from the *Review of Radical Political Economics* 4 (Spring 1972): R26–1–12.

Wright, Arthur W. "Discussion [of papers on the taxation of natural resources]." *American Economic Review* 65 (May 1975): 405–6.

PUBLIC DOCUMENTS

Barbados

Annual Statistical Digest. Bridgetown: Central Bank of Barbados, 1975.

Balance of Payments of Barbados, 1973. Bridgetown: Statistical Service, 1974.

Barrow, Errol W. *Supplementary Financial Statement and Budget Proposals*. Bridgetown: Government Printing Office, 1974.

Blackman, Courtney N. "Price Control within the Context of a Developing Economy." In *Central Bank of Barbados Quarterly Report* 3 (September 1976): 27–35.

Economic Survey 1968; 1971. Bridgetown: Economic Planning Unit, 1969; 1972.

Monthly Digest of Statistics. Bridgetown: Statistical Service, 1977.

Overseas Trade 1974. Bridgetown: Statistical Service, 1975.

Guyana

Annual Account Relating to External Trade 1974. Georgetown: Ministry of Economic Development, 1975.

Annual Statistical Abstract, 1974. Georgetown: Ministry of Economic Development, 1975.

British Guiana (Guyana) Development Programme (1966–1972). Georgetown: The Government Printery, 1966.

Budget 1976. Georgetown: Guyana Printers, 1975.

Economic Bulletin. Georgetown: Bank of Guyana, 1976.

Economic Survey of Guyana. Georgetown: Ministry of Economic Development, 1974.

Jamaica

Demographic Statistics. Kingston: Department of Statistics, 1976.

Economic and Social Survey Jamaica 1970 to 1975. Kingston: The Government Printer, 1971 to 1976.

External Trade, Annual Review 1974. Kingston: Department of Statistics, 1975.

External Trade, January–September 1975. Kingston: Department of Statistics, 1976.

Jamaica Bauxite Institute. *Jamaica and the Bauxite Companies: What the Agreements Mean.* Mimeographed. No date.

Jamaica Bauxite Institute. *Royalties, Income Taxes and the Bauxite Levy 1950–1976.* Mimeographed. No date.

JBI Digest 1 (1976).

Labour Force, The. Kingston: Department of Statistics, 1975, 1976.

National Income and Product 1976. Kingston: Department of Statistics, 1977.

Report and Statement of Accounts for the Year Ended 31st December 1971. Kingston: Bank of Jamaica, 1972.

Statistical Abstracts 1972 to 1976. Kingston: Department of Statistics, 1973 to 1977.

Statistical Digest. Kingston: Bank of Jamaica, 1976.

Trinidad and Tobago

Accounting for the Petrodollar. Port-of-Spain: Central Statistical Office, 1977.

Annual Statistical Digest 1973–74. Port-of-Spain: Central Statistical Office, 1975.

Balance of Payments of Trinidad and Tobago. Port-of-Spain: Central Statistical Office, 1975.

Chambers, G. M. *Budget Speech 1973*. Port-of-Spain: Government Printery, 1973.

Flow of Funds for Trinidad and Tobago, 1966–1974. Port-of-Spain: Central Statistical Office, 1977.

Gross Domestic Product of the Republic of Trinidad and Tobago 1966–1976. Port-of-Spain: Central Statistical Office, 1977.

Overseas Trade 1974. Port-of-Spain: Central Statistical Office, 1976.

Review of the Economy 1976. Port-of-Spain: Central Statistical Office, 1976.

Third Five-Year Plan 1969–1973 (draft). Port-of-Spain: Government Printery, 1969.

United States

Adelman, Irma. "Interaction of U.S. and Foreign Economic Growth Rates and Patterns." In *U.S. Economic Growth from 1976 to 1986: Prospects, Problems, and Patterns—Economic Growth in the International Context*, Vol. 12, pp. 1–15. Joint Economic Committee of the Congress of the United States. Washington: Government Printing Office, 1977.

Baer, Donald. "U.S.-Basin Imports: Structure and the GSP," in *Caribbean Basin Economic Survey* 3 (December 1977): 1–11.

Board of Governors, Federal Reserve System. *Federal Reserve Bulletin*.

Council on International Economic Policy. *Special Report: Critical Imported Materials*. Washington, D.C.: Government Printing Office, 1974.

Department of Commerce, Bureau of the Census. *U.S. General Imports—Schedule A Commodity by Country*. Washington, D.C.: Government Printing Office, 1978.

Department of Commerce. *U.S. Industrial Outlook 1978*. Washington, D.C.: Government Printing Office, 1977.

Department of Labor. *Immigrants and the American Labor Market*. Manpower Research Monograph No. 31. Washington, D.C.: Government Printing Office, 1974.

Economic Report of the President, 1978. Washington, D. C.: Government Printing Office, 1978.

Immigration and Naturalization Service, *Annual Reports 1962–76.* Washington, D.C.: Government Printing Office, 1963–77.

International Economic Report of the President. Washington, D.C.: Government Printing Office, 1977.

Joint Aluminum Copper Forecasting and Simulation Model. Report prepared for the U.S. Department of the Interior, Bureau of Mines, by Synergy, Inc., 1977.

Joint Economic Committee, Congress of the United States. *Achieving Price Stability through Economic Growth.* Washington, D.C.: Government Printing Office, 1974.

U.S. Economic Relations with Latin America. Hearings before the Subcommittee on Inter-American Economic Relationships of the Joint Economic Committee, Congress of the United States, 94th Cong., 2d sess. Washington, D.C.: Government Printing Office, 1977.

Valdez, Abelardo. "Statement before the Subcommittee on Inter-American Affairs, House of Representatives International Relations Committee." June 28, 1977. Mimeographed.

Vogley, William A. "Resource Substitution." In *U.S. Economic Growth from 1976 to 1986: Prospects, Problems, and Patterns—Resources and Energy,* Vol. 4, pp. 82–93. Joint Economic Committee of the Congress of the United States. Washington, D.C.: Government Printing Office, 1977.

International

Demas William G. "CDB: A Bank and a Development Instrument." Statement at the Seventh Annual Meeting of the Board of Governors, April 1977, Port-of-Spain.

International Monetary Fund. *International Financial Statistics* 3 (October 1977).

New Directions and New Structures for Trade and Development. Report by the Secretary-General of the United Nations Conference on Trade and Development to UNCTAD IV, TD/183/Rev. 1. New York: United Nations, 1977.

World Bank News Release. June 26, 1978.

World Tables, 1976. Washington: International Bank for Reconstruction and Development, 1977.

NEWSPAPERS AND MAGAZINES

Stone, Carl. "IMF Pressure Brought to Bear." *Jamaica Weekly Gleaner (NA)*. January 18, 1978, p. 8.

Stone, Carl. "Of Jobs and Politics." *Jamaica Weekly Gleaner (NA)*. July 3, 1978, p. 11.

Ward, Erskine, "The Industry Survives." *The Bajan*, December 1976, 18–20.

UNPUBLISHED PAPERS AND SPEECHES

Abrams, Franklin. "Immigration Law and Its Enforcement: Reflections of American Immigration." Paper presented at a conference sponsored by the Research Institute on Immigration and Ethnic Studies, Smithsonian Institution, Washington, D.C., November 1976.

Axline, W. Andrew. "Autonomy and Integration: The Issue of Caribbean International Relations," paper presented at the Seminar on Political and Economic Choices in the Contemporary Caribbean, Woodrow Wilson International Center for Scholars, Smithsonian Institution, February 1978, Washington, D.C.

Keleher, Robert E. "A Framework for Examining the Small, Open Regional Economy: An Application of the Macroeconomics of Open Systems." Paper presented at the Western Economic Association meetings, Honolulu, June 24, 1978.

Todman, Terence A. Keynote address at the 2nd Caribbean Conference on Trade, Investment and Development, Miami, January 19, 1978.